"Curiosity and courage are unstoppable forces. In this insightful book, Joanne Irving deftly shows how to enlist them to become a leader fit for the future."

— **Daniel H. Pink, #1 The New York Times bestselling author of WHEN and DRIVE**

"The book cover graphic of *The C² Factor for Leadership* is a trailer for this profound book. The magical power of leadership is the effective blend of the courage of a lion with the curiosity of a cat. This myth-busting book will alter your leadership perspectives and practices by providing cutting edge substance, compelling examples, and insightful tools."

— **Chip R. Bell, author of *Inside Your Customer's Imagination***

"Packed with nuggets of wisdom from the experiences of champion-level leaders across industries, Dr. Irving demonstrates how champion leaders engage their curiosity and courage to learn from the past, enhance the present, and anticipate the future."

— **Marshall Goldsmith, The New York Times #1 bestselling author of *Triggers, Mojo,* and *What Got You Here Won't Get You There* and Thinkers 50 #1 Executive Coach**

"Today's champion leaders learn to work in and through complexity, using curiosity to find the elements in the environment that they can change and then having the courage to do something about it. That is the C² Factor."

— **Jonah Berger, bestselling author of *Contagious* and *The Catalyst***

"If you're a leader – of a team, department, or organization – *The C² Factor* is for you. This accessible and engaging book enables you to see inside the decision-making process of top leaders, so you can hone your own strategic acumen."

— **Dorie Clark, author of *The Long Game* and Executive Education Faculty, Duke University Fuqua School of Business**

"Dr. Joanne Irving is an advisor to Washington, DC's power elite. For years, she's worked closely with heads of government, the military, and corporations on how to navigate challenges and lead with wisdom and grace. Few people understand, then, what it takes to lead in the real world better than Dr. Irving. If you and your organization are trying to accomplish something of magnitude, her new book *The C² Factor* is indispensable."

– Mark Levy, author of *Accidental Genius*, Levy Innovation: Differentiation for Corporations, Brands, and Thought Leaders

"This inspiring book illuminates how curiosity and courage can be leveraged by champion leaders across all industries to achieve new levels of creativity and collaboration within their organization, exponentially raising productivity and effective decision-making."

– Jennifer L. Farris, COO, Zuckerman Mind Brain Behavior Institute, Columbia University

"Through Joanne's newest work, *The C² Factor for Leadership*, Joanne helps companies take performance to even higher levels by exploring how leaders amplify their impact through the use of Courage and Curiosity. Joanne has an innate knack at helping companies and their leaders discover how these qualities can separate themselves from the competition."

– Rick Dudek, SVP Payer and Channel Access, Pfizer

"A thought-provoking read for leaders at every level who want to build healthy thriving organizations and enhance both their personal and professional lives. I am giving it to our leadership team to read."

– Beth Monroe, CEO, Justin Bradley, Washington, DC

"With a great mix of explanations, examples, and exercises, this engaging and energizing book brings a new and interesting focus to curiosity and courage. *The C² Factor for Leadership* is applicable to corporate/organizational leadership goals as well as one's personal life and community involvement. This book exceeded my expectations. It was the sort of page turner that I didn't expect."

– Elise Bolda, Ph.D., former Chair and Associate Professor Emerita Graduate Program in Public Health, Muskie School, USM

The C² Factor for Leadership

The C^2 Factor
for Leadership

How the Alchemy of Curiosity and Courage Helps Leaders Become Champions and Lead Meaningful Lives

Joanne Boyd Irving, Ph.D.

Routledge
Taylor & Francis Group

A PRODUCTIVITY PRESS BOOK

First published 2022
by Routledge
605 Third Avenue, New York, NY 10158

and by Routledge
4 Park Square, Milton Park, Abingdon, Oxon, OX14 4RN

Routledge is an imprint of the Taylor & Francis Group, an informa business

Library of Congress Cataloging-in-Publication Data
A catalog record for this title has been requested

ISBN: 9781032080888 (hbk)
ISBN: 9781032080840 (pbk)
ISBN: 9781003212881 (ebk)

DOI: 10.4324/9781003212881

Typeset in Minion
by Deanta Global Publishing Services, Chennai, India

Contents

Acknowledgments

Inspiration comes in so many forms, usually when we least expect it and in the most unlikely of ways. *"I'm just so curious about what comes next."* These were the poignant and profound last words of a dear colleague and friend as she lay in her hospital bed. A true champion, she was an early source of inspiration, guidance, and courage for me. I am grateful for her friendship, the model she exemplified, and for the many contributions of advisors, colleagues, clients, friends, and family who enriched my journey writing this book.

Alan Weiss set me on the path to being an expert consultant and to writing this book. He impressed upon me the idea that all quality consultants produce IP, pushing and guiding me to put fingers to keyboard and thoughts to the page. He and the many outstanding professionals in his community have inspired, challenged, and supported me through this entire process.

Constance Dierickx especially has been a steadfast mentor and colleague, whose thought-provoking ideas and energizing discussions have certainly widened and deepened my perspectives and knowledge.

My deepest appreciation to Debbie Jenkins, my stalwart cheerleader, coach and editor. Her indomitable spirit and tenacity through a year of Zoom calls helping me wrestle concepts into a proposal is nothing short of extraordinary. As I grappled with writing, she picked me up when I was down, and somehow convinced me I was the "real deal" with something important to say when doubt got the better of me. She galvanized my thinking, held me accountable, but never shamed me when I didn't produce what I'd committed to so I was able to persevere and make progress. Thank you, Debs.

Words cannot express my profound gratitude for all the ways Anita Galloway Mooy helped me with this book. With her intellect, sense of humor, and seemingly infinite patience, she helped me clarify and articulate my thoughts over many lengthy phone calls. She helped me find the right words to say what I was trying to say. Having her feedback and input is what gives me the confidence to show this book to the world.

Her participation in this project is truly what made it not only possible, but often sheer joy.

Special thanks to Mary Beth Merrin and Janice Mandel who when intrigued by my idea, seeded the process with introductions that eventually led to interviews with so many champion leaders. Sincere thanks to the 62 champion leaders who so graciously took time from their extremely busy schedules to share with me their experiences of how curiosity and courage contributed to their enormous success. And, to my wonderful clients who have given me so many opportunities to learn and who demonstrate their champion leadership daily.

Thank you to my beta readers, Beth Monroe, Elise Boda, and Pam Holland who provided thoughtful and useful feedback when I was too close to have perspective.

And, last, but most certainly not least are my husband and sons. My sons for asking repeatedly about my progress and for Channing's unwavering confidence in and support of me, his tolerance of my long work hours, and the many, many dinners he prepared! Thank you, my loves. I will be eternally grateful.

About the Author

 Working at the intersection of business and psychology, Joanne Irving, Ph.D., helps influential and accomplished leaders improve professional and business outcomes, organizational performance, and the quality of life for themselves and those around them.

A leadership expert who specializes in helping CEOs and senior executives at large and mid-sized companies, Joanne has advised executives at some of the world's most successful organizations, including the World Bank, the International Monetary Fund, the Federal Department of Defense, Johnson & Johnson, Microsoft, Pfizer, AARP, Atlantic Health Systems, and General Electric, to name but a few.

For over three decades, Joanne's clients have been consistently recognized for their achievements, increased influence, and ability to lead in the most challenging times. They inspire people to excel and achieve extraordinary results.

Joanne graduated *summa cum laude* from Tufts University; received her Ph.D. in psychology from the University of Maryland; and conducted her internship at Johns Hopkins University Hospital.

Introduction

We live in turbulent times, enduring constant and rapid changes in everything from technology to social, economic, environmental, and geopolitical domains. Leading today requires more than a high IQ and EQ to navigate an ever-shifting landscape of tumult and uncertainty. It requires curiosity and courage, but not simply those traits in their raw form. It is the alchemy of the two, the synergistic application of profound curiosity and relentless courage that has the power to help us thrive as leaders, as team members, as partners, and as individuals. This superpower is the C^2 Factor.

How can we prepare for a future when COVID reminds us of just how surprised we are when it arrives? There is no way to accurately predict the future. There is no field manual for leadership for what is to come. Best practices don't apply. Yet leaders still need to lead.

Models of exceptional leadership typically focus on cognitive skills such as business competence, creating a vision, and strategic thinking; and emotional intelligence such as communicating, inspiring, and developing others. These traits are necessary but insufficient for leadership today. Leadership development programs that emphasize building skills become sadly out of date almost immediately.

Books providing formulas for organizational success consist of good ideas that have worked in other organizations in the past, but there is no guarantee that they are appropriate for yours today. Relationship advice and self-help books are too often simplistic and based merely on the author's personal experience.

- What is crucial for thriving in this complex, rapidly changing world?
- How can we build and sustain organizations that not only deliver financial success but also serve their stakeholders, their employees, and even society as a whole?
- How do we identify needed change, create a vision, and take action in the face of uncertainty?
- How do we create an organizational culture that is innovative and agile at its very core?

- What will keep our personal and professional relationships vibrant?
- What will engender satisfaction and fulfillment in our personal lives?

With over 30 years of experience working with influential and accomplished leaders across the country helping them improve business outcomes and the quality of life for themselves and those around them, I have often asked these questions. As I reflected on those leaders who were most transformative, most able to seize the moment, and the most caring and wise, I realized that they all had two qualities in common – they are remarkably curious and courageous.

To test my hypothesis, I interviewed 62 additional leaders – names you may have heard of and plenty of unknown, champion leaders who are quietly changing their world. Their candid insights, ability to reflect and extrapolate, plus their willingness to share what's gone well and what's not worked for them helped me develop my thinking.

Working at the intersection of psychology and business, I recognized that beyond skills, beyond IQ and EQ, these leaders have personality characteristics that enable them to respond to changes regardless of what those changes are. Today's world is different from what tomorrow will bring, so business as usual does not work. To embrace and exploit the future, we need to develop and exercise the C^2 Factor – the application of profound curiosity and relentless courage, continuously oscillating between them.

Curiosity and courage both are requisite attitudes and deliberate behaviors that can be described, practiced, and strengthened. When they are truly combined, they enhance and are enhanced by each other. What distinguishes transformative leaders, what separates the champion leaders from the pack, is their profound curiosity and their relentless courage – the C^2 Factor.

To be successful and, just as importantly, to sustain fulfilling lives, leaders must ask questions and make decisions that challenge, even defy conventional wisdom. They must examine themselves, their assumptions, beliefs, and attitudes. They must take action to respond to conditions they have never anticipated. They must exercise their C^2 Factor.

It is the best of times and the worst of times. We live in a complex, interconnected world marked by rapid changes in technology, social/political disruption, threats to the environment, and a global on-demand market. There is no doubt that developments in artificial intelligence, robotics, virtual reality, biologic sensors, and 3D printing, to name just a few technology frontiers, will present unanticipated opportunities and challenges. Increased awareness of gender and racial bias, inequitable income and resource distribution, and demand for universal healthcare provide the backdrop and create a milieu ripe for unforeseen shifts in how we navigate our world. Added to the mix are turbulent changes in the natural environment, an increasingly matrixed geopolitical world, and most recently a global pandemic.

So, no doubt there will be another VUCA[1] event to which we will need to respond personally, in our relationships and as leaders. Trying to guess "the answer" is a fool's game because it is illusive. Technical skills are easily outdated. We need to be able to dance in the moment, responding to change and finding ways to help ourselves and those around us thrive. That will require the synergistic application of curiosity and courage, the C^2 Factor.

There's no individual person that the C^2 Factor can't positively impact; no two-person relationship that it wouldn't improve; no team, no organization that wouldn't benefit from members with their C^2 Factor ignited. When we look at the world with curiosity, there is so much to know. And when we have courage, there is so much to do!

NOTE

1. It is an acronym introduced by the U.S. Army War College to describe the more volatile, uncertain, complex and ambiguous world as a result of the end of the Cold War.

1

The Myths You May Believe about Curiosity and Courage that Can Lead You Astray

We are all susceptible to believing myths and making assumptions based on those beliefs. Courage and curiosity were unquestionably vivid, bold character strengths of the 62 elite champion leaders I spoke with, but often they did not recognize these traits in themselves. Their assumptions, many based on prevalent myths, limited their ability to see what was so evident in their personal and professional lives. Without clarity and knowledge of our character strengths, we are less able to access them, develop them, and deliberately deploy them. Debunking these myths helps us more deeply understand curiosity and courage, the various ways they are manifested, and how to identify these traits in ourselves.

It was the middle of the night when my mother called to tell me that, once again, my brother had been arrested for drug possession. His child was about to be placed in foster care. I was just 22 years old, from an indigenous culture, and the first of my family to go to college. I was struggling to adjust to academic demands and the social pressures of a more urban life. To say that I was stressed is an understatement, but I knew what I needed to do. I adopted my brother's daughter, voluntarily becoming a single mother at 22.

The CEO of a global manufacturing company told me this story during our conversation about her leadership journey. Most would agree that what she did took enormous courage; however, when I asked her if she

DOI: 10.4324/9781003212881-1

thought of herself as courageous, she said, "Courageous? I don't know if I'd call myself courageous. I guess I think of myself as strong."

Similarly, another leader, the president and CEO of a hospitality company responsible for turning her local business into a national powerhouse catering premiere events like the U.S. Tennis Open, did not recognize curiosity in herself. When asked, she replied, "Curious? I really don't think I am. I guess I'd call myself inquisitive." Clearly, neither executive recognized the traits of courage or curiosity in themselves.

Although courage and curiosity are character strengths that are integral to the stories of many successful leaders, they often appear in a seemingly unconscious way. I interviewed 62 executives – all champion leaders, all extraordinarily curious and courageous, but, surprisingly, many of them didn't realize it. These leaders are CEOs, COOs, CIOs, Presidents, Senior Vice Presidents, General Managers, Executive Directors, and Judges, to name but a few. They come from organizations ranging from manufacturing to pharmaceutical companies, to the biggest names in Silicon Valley, to banking and nonprofit associations. Our conversations helped them recognize what they sometimes hadn't noticed about themselves and helped me appreciate the nuances of both curiosity and courage in the leadership journey.

Recognition of character traits like courage and curiosity can have a profound impact on our professional and personal lives. When we recognize these traits, or personal assets, they become more available for use. Our self-image is a major determinant of our behavior. When faced with a challenging situation, a person who thinks of themselves as courageous and curious will face it head-on, looking for all the nuances and opportunities and then take action. Whereas someone who doesn't believe They have those traits may keep their head down, avoid conflict, focus on the immediate task, and hope it goes away. Being aware that we possess these traits is the essential first step in further developing them. We can also help others in our lives recognize these traits in themselves and further build their courage and curiosity "muscles." This is how champion leaders build organizations filled with curious, courageous, effective teams.

Perhaps the reason some of the leaders I interviewed didn't recognize these qualities was that they had assumptions that limited their ability to see what, to me, was so clear about their personalities and their lives. Many of those assumptions were borne out of prevalent myths about curiosity and courage. Examining a few of these myths will deepen our appreciation and understanding of these character strengths so that we can tap into them when we need them and further develop these capacities.

FOUR MYTHS ABOUT CURIOSITY THAT MUDDLE YOUR UNDERSTANDING

Myth 1: You Either Are or Are Not Curious

To be human is to be curious. We are all born curious. The famous infant psychologist, Harry Harlow[1] (1950) was one of the first in a continuing line of scientists who consider curiosity a basic human drive, as necessary for survival as nourishment and touch.

Curiosity is essential for cognitive and emotional development. Infants as young as two months old show a distinct preference for novel patterns over familiar ones. Toddlers want to touch everything, go everywhere, and put everything in their mouths. By age four, children constantly ask "why?" Considered an intrinsic motivation, curiosity is the driving force that propels the growing child to learn about the world around them. So, the idea that a human being is not curious by nature is simply not true.

Curiosity can be thought of as a character trait in that individuals differ in the amount of curiosity they demonstrate. From birth we all differ in what is called "sensation seeking." Some of us are born actively embracing all forms of new stimuli, while others are more reluctant. This suggests that there may be a biological basis for some differences in curiosity.

One community college president told me, "Curiosity is part of my DNA. As a kid, I was the one always asking questions. I sometimes joke that I never left the three-year-old stage, asking 'Why? Why? Why?'" But the desire to seek out something new grows or shrinks depending on the response of people around the developing child. Curiosity may be inhibited by well-meaning adults trying to protect the child from danger or teach the appropriate behavior for the culture or it can be nourished so that it flourishes. It is largely our experiences throughout our lives that contribute to our curiosity's growth or decline.

Former CIA officer, diplomat, and White House Advisor, Yael Eisenstat, who now heads a global risk firm, told me how her mother had supported her curiosity (and courage). When she was 14 years old, living in a very posh town in California, she wanted to see what was outside of her bubble and write about the town just north of where she lived, East Palo Alto, then the murder capital of the United States. She wanted to experience other parts of the world. She explained, "My mother definitely did not clip my wings. She encouraged me to explore. She let me go overseas at fifteen. I think that was really the start of knowing there was a broader world that I had to be a part of."

Curiosity is also a "state." Depending on the circumstances, people will be more or less curious. Different situations can dictate whether or not a person acts with curiosity. The particular subject matter, the degree of novelty, and the degree of challenge all determine how curious a person will be in any given situation.

Research indicates that when we experience an optimal level of novelty, meaning it is just within reach of our capacity to manage, we are most curious. If something is too novel, we are not interested because we have no context for understanding it or because it feels overwhelming. For example, I have no interest in attending a lecture on astrophysics because I don't know enough about the subject to be curious.

One executive I interviewed told me that when she first came to the United States as a young girl, she stayed in her room as much as possible because she was overwhelmed by just how much she didn't understand. It was later, when she tapped into her curiosity and courage, that she began her journey to becoming the CEO of a well-respected company in Silicon Valley.

So, if you want to spark your own curiosity, get a little information. Learn something about a topic you know nothing about. Listen to people around you who know about something you don't. And be aware that if you want to spark other people's curiosity for your idea, encourage their questions before sharing your thoughts fully, and be sure to provide just enough novelty, being mindful not to overwhelm them.

Myth 2: We Should Emulate 3-Year-Olds

Often romanticized, curiosity is frequently listed as an admirable trait of accomplished people and lauded by organizations that profess a desire for curiosity to flourish. To enhance our lives, we are implored to cultivate the "wonder of a young child." But emulating the curiosity of a 3-year-old is much too simplistic a notion to be very useful. "Not all curiosity is good,"

Cara Lesser, founder and CEO of the Kid Museum, an organization built on encouraging youth to follow their curiosity, noted to my surprise. "Last week my nephew swallowed a marble just to see what it would be like."

Three-year-olds have wandering curiosity. They move from one new thing to the next. This kind of curiosity is integral to learning and development, but it is not without its shortcomings. As any parent will tell you, it is scattered and unfocused and unfettered, it can be dangerous. Built on the early wandering curiosity of the toddler, "diversive" curiosity inspires us to scan the environment for interesting things – unexpected events, changes in our surroundings, something novel to us in any form. While "specific" curiosity drives us like scholars and scientists to deepen our understanding of a particular subject. Both are valuable.

"I wanted to stir the curiosity of the team to go above and beyond what they needed to know from their professional reading," Bonnie Fogel, Executive Director of Imagination Stage told me. She encouraged her leadership team to read extensively and once a month she asked one of them to present something that they had read that particularly influenced them. She said:

> If an organization is going to be successful, the leaders need to be continu-
> ally looking outside their own edges and be curious about the world, trying
> to figure out if there something happening that we will need to know about
> and how can what's happening inform our practices.

Curiosity comes in many forms. It is not only the type demonstrated by young children. Kashdan et al.,[2] for example, identified six types of curiosity: joyous exploration, deprivation sensitivity, stress tolerance, thrill seeking, and social (which he later subdivided into overt and covert social curiosity). Drawing on work by Berlyne, Silva, Kashdan,[3] and Lowenstein, Ian Leslie notes that the types of curiosity can be differentiated based on what motivates it and on what satisfies it. Is it provoked by something that is a surprise or novel or is it because we are trying to develop knowledge and understanding? Or is it just a way to avoid boredom? Will it be satisfied by specific answers and solutions, or is the goal to acquire deep knowledge?

Curiosity can be manifested in many ways. Figure 1.1 shows the types of curiosity based on its depth, its focus, its motivation, and its direction. Bonnie Fogel encouraged broad curiosity about ideas in the world for the joy of knowing. Whereas I want my doctor to have specific curiosity about

Types of Curiosity

<u>Direction</u>

- Self
- Other people
- The physical world

<u>Depth</u>

- Deep, specific, detailed
- Wide, broad, general

<u>Focus</u>

- Ideas, facts
- Emotions, feelings
- Physical sensations

<u>Motivation</u>

- Joy of exploring
- Knowledge gap

FIGURE 1.1
Types of curiosity.

facts regarding my condition in order to bridge any gaps he might have in his knowledge.

The types of curiosity we can have go beyond that exhibited by a 3-year-old. We need to recognize the many ways it shows up in ourselves and others so that we can both nurture it and harvest its benefits.

Myth 3: School Is a Wet Blanket

In one of the most watched TED talks of all time, Fellow of the Royal Society of Arts, Sir Ken Robinson[4] argued that school kills creativity and suppresses curiosity. There is certainly reason to be concerned about how "teaching to the test" or emphasizing rote learning dampens curiosity. That said, we should not throw the baby out with the bath water. Knowledge gained through education provides the very spark that can ignite and fan the flames of curiosity.

Lowenstein,[5] a psychologist and behavior economist at Carnegie Mellon, believed that curiosity is an innate drive that arises from an information gap between what we know and what we want to know. He proposed that information fuels curiosity by creating awareness of ignorance. We cannot be curious about something that we are totally ignorant about.

Ian Leslie,[6] author of *Curious: The Desire to Know and Why Your Future Depends on It* (2014), notes that many inventions folklore attributes to serendipity and curiosity would not exist had the inventors not had vast knowledge of their field of study. Two such inventions are the microwave oven and penicillin. Percy Spencer, a scientist studying radiation in the Raytheon labs, noticed when he stood too close to vacuum tubes that create microwaves, the chocolate bar in his pocket melted, leading him to invent the microwave oven. Alexander Fleming noticed that mold in a petri dish kept bacteria from growing, which led him to the invention of penicillin. Their deep knowledge of their field prepared these scientists to be ready to spot and see the significance in what they were observing. Quoting Louis Pasteur, "Chance favors the prepared mind."

There is a feedback loop between knowledge and curiosity. Not only can knowledge stimulate curiosity, but curiosity also leads to increased knowledge and enhanced academic performance. Von Stumm,[7] a well-respected professor of psychology in education, reviewed the research on individual differences in academic performance. She evaluated 200 studies with over 50,000 students and concluded that intellectual curiosity was a strong predictor of academic achievement. Neurologists have found the brain mechanisms responsible for curiosity contribute to consolidation of learning and enhancing long-term memory.

YY Lee is a compelling example of this loop between knowledge and curiosity. In immigrating to this country as a child, she and her family had to take an evolutionary journey of curiosity entwined with gaining knowledge and formal education in order to rebuild their lives from the ground up in a new country. That journey required learning everything from a new language and culture to navigating often unwelcoming and dehumanizing work situations as well as finding ways to get both an academic and a social education.

YY Lee was (and is) tenaciously curious, which means she learns a lot, which in turn makes her more curious. Early on, she was extremely curious about technology and became a self-taught programmer, finding access to information and equipment to learn about emerging technologies which, eventually, was crucial in being able to support her education and launch her career. Her exhaustive use of the curiosity–knowledge loop is what propelled her to and through Harvard and is, more than anything else, the core of her success as a CEO, COO, public board member, General

Manager, and product leader across a variety of companies from start-ups to global divisions of major public companies. She credits her success to "my need, desire, and delight in understanding."

When it comes to curiosity, ignorance is not bliss! One needn't come from a school with a prestigious name, but it is important to recognize that education, knowledge, is the bedrock for curiosity.

Become aware of holes you may have in your knowledge. For example, how well do you understand world history? U.S. history? Allow your curiosity to lead you to increase your knowledge. Develop a broader world//cultural/political/social view. Go to the opera (but first read a little about it). Activities outside your usual scope will make you a more interesting person, able to appreciate the finer things, and perhaps ask more meaningful questions at your next meeting. Surround yourself – at work and at home – with people who have educated curiosity.

Myth 4: Curiosity Is a Waste of Time

We seem to be ambivalent about curiosity. On the one hand, it is romanticized in the form of the wonder child who wants to know everything about everything, and popular media eschews it as the source of creativity and innovation. On the other hand, it can be viewed as a waste of time or even a dangerous endeavor. Professionals with too much curiosity may be labeled as having "time management" or "productivity" issues. In some instances, the curiosity may even be pathologized and attributed to attention deficit disorder or ADD.

The idea that indulging curiosity is a dangerous endeavor is easily found reflected in such myths as the tale of Pandora opening a box containing sickness or the story of Adam and Eve. It may even be found in modern-day children's books such as the popular tales of "Curious George" and his mischief.

And, while it's true that folks with ADD get bored and there is some evidence that curiosity can lead adolescents to take risks, the preponderance of scientific findings reveals that curiosity actually leads to better decision-making. Curiosity results in fewer errors because more information is gathered, and more alternatives are considered. And in at least one study, "diversive" curiosity was positively correlated with both solution quality and originality beyond established predictors of creative performance, thereby forming the basis for innovation. Bonnie Fogel told me that it was her curiosity about an employee's girlfriend's aspirations that led to developing an entirely new aspect of the Imagination Stage, which later became core to their mission.

In conversations with leaders who are members of groups minoritized via racial, gender, sexual orientation, nationality, or generational biases, they explained that not only was curiosity *not* a waste of time, but, for them, it was also an essential skill for survival in a majority culture. These leaders referred to "environmental curiosity" explaining it as their need and ability to investigate everything in a situation so that they might fully understand what was "really going on."

For the purposes of this book, curiosity is defined as having an open and seeking mind, an eagerness to learn. It is the recognition, pursuit, and intense desire to explore novel, challenging, and uncertain situations. It takes on several different forms and does not necessarily diminish after childhood, but rather continues to contribute to achievement and expertise.

When faced with challenging situations, we must access our curiosity. We must seize opportunities to indulge and cultivate our curiosity and the curiosity of those around us. If we consciously decide what role we want curiosity to play in our lives, it will contribute to our achievement and expertise.

FOUR MYTHS ABOUT COURAGE THAT DEFEAT YOUR ATTITUDE

Myth 1: Courage Is the Same as Fearlessness

This myth is easily dismissed by the common definition of courage as taking action despite fear. However, the question of fear and courage is still hotly debated among scholars. Many definitions of courage include fearlessness as a necessary component. One study hypothesized that courage may be defined by the observer's sense that they would be afraid in a particular situation.

So, if it's not fearlessness, what is courage? Most scientific research on courage has focused on trying to find the answer to that question. A 2007 article in the *Journal of Positive Psychology* investigating the concept of courage reported finding well over 29 different definitions of courage. My review of current research suggests that courage has four components: (1) a willingness to take action after some assessment (2) for a worthy goal (3) in the face of risk (4) when the outcome is uncertain.

While Ana Pinczuk was in a development position at Bell Laboratories in the United States, she was unexpectedly invited to move to an AT&T sales role for wireless in South America. "The only thing I had going for me was that I spoke Spanish. Wireless was new. I didn't know the market or sales. I was going into a culture that was traditionally male dominated." Despite the personal risks, the organizational risks, and the uncertain outcome, Ana, now the Chief Development Officer at Anaplan, had the courage to take the leap to create something new for her organization. She is a superb example of a champion leader who has been courageous and was recently listed as number 11 on Forbes 50 Most Powerful Latinas in Business Roundup.

Courage is not about being impulsive. It is about taking action to achieve a worthy goal after being reflective about the risks involved. The risks may be personal – to one's reputation or financial status, for example – or they may be risks to others, such as one's organization and its employees. The risks may be very high. Nonetheless, despite uncertain outcome and no guarantee of success, the action is taken.

Are you the kind of leader who makes these determinations and who is willing to risk your reputation and perhaps the fate of others for a worthy goal? If so, you are likely a champion.

Myth 2: You Either Are or You Are Not Courageous

This myth suggests that courage is a singular character trait that a person either has or doesn't have – 24 hours a day, 7 days a week, 365 days a year in every situation. In fact, courage is complex and multidimensional. It doesn't show up the same way in all people or in all circumstances.

One way to think about courage is in terms of what is at risk if you take action. Physical courage, the willingness to put oneself at risk for bodily harm, was the earliest way we thought about courage and possibly the most obvious. The image of the man running into a burning building to save a child comes easily to mind or the courage of the soldier facing dangerous situations.

But there are many other types of courage. One way to think about courage is in terms of the arena in which it takes place. We mentioned physical courage above. Intellectual courage is the willingness to risk making mistakes or questioning a well-established concept. Emotional courage is the willingness to feel the full spectrum of our feelings, including the ones we may not be proud of. Perhaps the greatest form of courage is moral courage: the willingness to stand up when an ethical standard – honesty, integrity, fairness, respect, loyalty, etc. – is being violated.

If we look at courage from the standpoint of what is at risk when we act courageously, we see that we can risk our physical safety whether it's bodily harm or economic well-being. We can risk our social status, being subject to rejection or ridicule. And we can risk our psychological health – our self-esteem, confidence, etc.

Finally, we can think about courage by considering who benefits from the action. Will the action achieve a personal objective, or will it benefit another individual? Or will the action benefit the "greater good?" If so, what is your definition of "greater good?" Is the "greater good" your family, your organization, or society as a whole? The beneficiaries needn't be mutually exclusive. Many actions benefit more than one individual or group.

The different elements of each dimension of courage are summarized in Figure 1.2. Note that these are not mutually exclusive.

Dimensions of Courage

Challenge or Cause

<u>Physical</u>	<u>Intellectual</u>	<u>Emotional</u>	<u>Moral</u>
Strength	Ideas Thoughts Beliefs	Feelings	Ethics

What is at Risk

<u>Physical safety</u>	<u>Social Status</u>	<u>Psychological health</u>
Bodily harm Financial security	Rejection Embarrassment	Self esteem Confidence

Beneficiaries

<u>Self</u>	<u>Specific Others</u>	<u>The Organization</u>	<u>Society/the World</u>

FIGURE 1.2
Dimensions of courage.

One example of courage is a story told to me by a senior executive at an organization that oversees over $160 billion in assets. Her story demonstrates how she faced a challenge, taking action because she very much believed it was a worthy endeavor even though there was great personal risk to her career and risk to the company if she did not take a stand. She knew going in there was a big chance she would fail, but she also knew she must act in a manner that aligned with her professional ethics.

"Very early in my career when I was just 25, I worked for a large, family-owned investment bank. The firm had a trust, and I was the lawyer for the trust company. A matter arose and I determined we could not take the proposed action. The boss, whose surname also graced the company, believed we could and should take that action. I was told he wanted to speak to me, but I knew he wanted to convince me to agree with him.

My knees were knocking, and I was really afraid. I knew that opposing him was taking a considerable risk, but I also knew it was the right thing for me to do and the right thing for the company.

I sat in front of his immense desk as he intimidatingly perched on the front edge of it looking down at me and began telling me why we needed to do x, y, and z.

I responded, "But Mr. _____, we really can't do it for these reasons."

"Are you telling me we can't do it?" he questioned me. I reaffirmed we could not.

"Are you sure? You're telling me we can't do it," he questioned again. I replied, "I'm sure."

Then he said "Okay. Then we won't do it."

And he went back to the other side of the desk. I said, "Oh, can I go now?"

He said, "No, no stay. Do you know how many people there are in this institution that will tell me no?"

As I waited for what I felt was an imminent firing, I said, "I don't know."

But to my surprise, he said "One!! And it's you! I like you, young lady, you are going to go far."

We then had a really good talk and from that day forward he made a point to speak to me at company events. Years later after I had worked my way up in the company, he said, "you know, I never forgot you telling me no because people are always saying yes to me. I got into the habit of just bullying people into saying yes, but you have so much respect for someone when they don't. You must always do that. That will be the secret sauce in your career."

When faced with a challenge, it can be useful to ask oneself:

- Is this challenge worthy of facing?
- What risks are involved?
- Who benefits from success?
- What are the chances of a successful outcome?
- How will I feel about myself based on the action I take?

Myth 3: Courage Is Always Recognized

The word "courage" often evokes images of large heroic acts – exceptional people acting in extraordinary ways. Indeed, there are some truly inspirational examples of such courage. Scott McClelland, the president of grocery store H-E-B's Houston division, is a great example of this kind of heroic courage. When Category 4 Hurricane Harvey slammed into the Houston, Texas area, he managed to keep 60 stores open so that people could have the supplies they needed to ride out the disaster.

We often think of leadership courage as making bold moves on behalf of their organization, but as vulnerability researcher and author Brene Brown[8] asserts, champion leaders also demonstrate tremendous courage when they are willing to be vulnerable.

One example of this type of courage and willingness to be vulnerable is the story of Annette Parker, the first African-American President of South Central College in Minnesota. Upon arrival at the college, she had to immediately tackle some long-standing, entrenched personnel issues. After a thorough investigation, she took action. She was criticized viciously by some members of the faculty and endured difficult, false accusations and challenging confrontations. But, she told me, she survived with her integrity. She held her head up high and had the courage to walk the halls and lead, as she told me, "Through the process of healing."

There are also the many small everyday acts that require courage but are not so publicly visible. Taking responsibility for a project that went wrong, speaking up for someone who is being unfairly maligned, going to school when you don't speak the language that is being spoken are also examples of courage. Audrey Fauvel left her high-level corporate position as General Manager at Deutsche Bank, Europe, to start a small fintech company to support women entrepreneurs. During our conversation, I had to point out to her that this was an act of courage.

We often overlook or dismiss acts of courage in our private lives as well. Courage may take the form of having difficult, vulnerable conversations with partners, dealing with the bad behavior of a child, confronting an addiction, or working to overcome symptoms of emotional issues. All of these actions are forms of courage that are less visible but no less easy to exhibit.

Are you looking for all the opportunities in your life to be courageous?

Myth 4: Courage Can't be Learned

Unlike curiosity, humans are not born with courage. What seems like the toddler's courage to do almost anything is, as a nanny once told me, "Because they have no sense. They get afraid when they have sense," she explained. Psychologists and neuroscientists tell us that some individuals have an inborn trait that enjoys risk, but there is no indication that they are more likely to be courageous. So how do some people become more courageous than others?

Courage is learned. It is learned by watching our role models. Many of the leaders I spoke to talked about the courage their immigrant parents modeled. Ann Breen-Greco, a Judge for the City of Chicago Illinois State Board of Education, spoke of her mother coming to the United States from Ireland as an indentured servant because there was no opportunity for her in Ireland.

Jennifer Lin, SVP/CPO at Trimble, told me about the courage of her parents in coming to the United States from South Korea in 1957 without knowing anyone. When I asked Jennifer, a former Google executive, where she got her courage, she told me, "My mother – she did not know anyone in the US and came to the states despite her mother's advice to 'just marry a nice husband and stay here (Korea) and live comfortably.'" Jennifer added, "She independently explored new frontiers and set the ultimate example, which inspired courage in her children."

Small acts of courage help us build that muscle. When we are placed or place ourselves in situations that call for action despite risk and we step up to the challenge, we increase our confidence to take that kind of action again. Acting courageously creates an internal experience of courage and reinforces that sense of self. By practicing courage, we become courageous.

As Sandie Okoro, Senior Vice-President and Group General Counsel for the World Bank, told me, "Courage is like a muscle. You train it by taking the first step. It gets easier."

I asked Darley Newman how she had the courage to make the world's highest commercial bungee jump, or trek the world's highest climbing wall, or swim with sharks. Surprisingly, the entrepreneur, adventurer, and producer of Emmy Award-winning documentaries said that perhaps her mother's demand that she sing in front of family guests when she was very young contributed to her ability to undertake courageous adventures as an adult.

Developing other character strengths also helps build courage. Traits that have been associated with courage include self-confidence, openness to experience, perseverance, and endurance. It was striking how many of the champion leaders I interviewed took on assignments for which they felt underqualified. They were willing to do something risky because, although they didn't know how things would turn out, they believed that somehow, they would "figure things out."

The words "curiosity" and "courage" conjure up different images for different people. Many commonly held beliefs about curiosity and courage are not confirmed by facts. Curiosity, characterized as having an open and seeking mind, takes on several different forms and does not necessarily diminish after childhood, but rather continues to contribute to achievement and expertise. Courage is not the same as fearlessness. It is the ability to take action in the face of uncertainty or perceived danger in order to achieve a worthy goal. Courage is developed through encouragement from role models and strengthened by being courageous.

While understanding these personality traits separately is a useful beginning, it is the alchemy of them, the C^2 Factor, that strengthens our leadership and improves the quality of life for ourselves and those around us. The C^2 Factor is the signature characteristic of champion leaders who not only lead well now but are best prepared to lead us into the future.

NOTES

1. Harlow, H.F., Harlow, M.K., and Meyer, D.R. "Learning Motivated by a Manipulation Drive." *Journal of Experimental Psychology* 40 (1950): 228–234.
2. Kashdan, Todd B., Disabato, David J., Goodman, Fallon R., and Naughton, Carl. "The Five Dimensions of Curiosity." *Harvard Business Review*, September/October 2018.

3. Kashdan, Todd B., Disabato, David J., Goodman, Fallon R., Naughton, Carl, and McKnight, Patrick E. "The Five-Dimensional Curiosity Scale Revised (5DCR): Briefer Subscales while Separating Overt and Covert Curiosity." *Personality and Individual Differences* 157 (April 2020): 109836. https://doi.org/10.1016/j.paid.2020. 109836.

4. https://www.ted.com/talks/sir_ken_robinson_do_schools_kill_creativity.

5. Lowenstein, George. "The Psychology of Curiosity: A Review and Reinterpretation." *Psychology Bulletin* 116, no. 1 (1994): 75–98.

6. Lesley, Ian. *Curious.* New York: Basic Books, 2014.

7. Von Stumm, Sophie, Hell, Benedikt, and Chamorro-Premuzic, Tomas. "The Hungry Mind: Intellectual Curiosity Is the Third Pillar of Academic Performance." *Perspectives on Psychological Science.* First Published October 14, 2011. https://doi. org/10.1177/1745691611421204.

8. Brown, Brene. *Daring Greatly: How the Courage to Be Vulnerable Transforms the Way We Live, Love, Parent, and Lead.* New York: Avery Books, 2011.

2

The Alchemy of Curiosity and Courage

People can be curious without being courageous and courageous without being curious. But what happens when a person uses both of these traits simultaneously? When these two interdependent traits are combined, we see the true difference between champion leaders and merely adequate leaders. Exploring the four types of leaders based on the use of these traits helps us understand the impact (and potential pitfalls) inherent in engaging curiosity and courage while taking the self-assessment can help you identify your type of leadership.

Badgers and coyotes don't look like they'd be friends. Badgers are squat furry creatures with short legs, stumpy tails, and flat bodies. Coyotes have long legs, slender snouts, large pointed ears, and bushy tails. Coyotes are often mistaken for dogs. Badgers? More like furry anteaters. At first glance, curiosity and courage may not look much like they go together either.

Badgers and coyotes seem like they might be enemies. They live in the same area and hunt for the same kind of food – gophers, ground squirrels, moles, woodrats, deer mice, and voles. You might think they would compete for the prey, just as you might think curiosity and courage might compete in our minds.

In fact, the opposite is true. Badgers and coyotes are symbiotic – they have an interdependent relationship. Because they have different hunting styles, their prey reacts to them very differently. A ground squirrel dives into its hole when it sees a coyote and there, waiting for it, is the badger. On the other hand, if a ground squirrel encounters a badger in its hole, it will climb out to use its speed to outrun the badger. But it cannot outrun the coyote. Either way, the prey doesn't stand a chance. Just as the badger and the coyote are symbiotic, so too are curiosity and courage.

DOI: 10.4324/9781003212881-2

The synergy and symbiotic relationship between curiosity and courage produces an alchemy, the C² Factor.

In my interviews with champion executives, I was struck by how quickly those who identified either curiosity or courage as primary in their leadership journey began to talk about the other element as well. Given that curiosity and courage are symbiotic aspects of our personalities, each benefiting from the other, that should not be surprising. These traits are often so closely connected that they can be difficult to differentiate. Sometimes a leader told a story that I thought was about one, but it turned out to be about the other.

> I was working in a manufacturing facility when I heard a loud explosion and saw a man run by my door. His clothes were shredded and smoking, and he was calling for help. Without thinking, I ran blindly into the electrical substation where someone was tangled in electrical wires, literally on fire. I used the fire extinguisher then pulled him out to wait for help to arrive.

I thought it was an amazing story about courage that this former President and CEO of Coca Cola Bottler's Sales and Service, Gary Kapusta, had told me until he went on: "People were appreciative, naturally, and called me a hero, but at the time I really didn't feel courageous. I was motivated by my curiosity. I wanted to know what happened. I got up to see what was going on."

I don't know if I agree with Gary's assessment that there wasn't any courage involved in that incident (although perhaps the lack of consideration of the risk means it doesn't meet our criteria). The behavior of the now COO of II-VI does show how curiosity and courage are closely related in motivating people's behavior. Just as the badger and the coyote benefit from each other's presence, quiet curiosity can inspire fast-moving courage.

Curiosity and courage are more than symbiotic. They are also synergistic, meaning they potentiate or intensify each other. Synergy refers to the benefits generated when two agents combine and interact, achieving results beyond what either could achieve alone.

Business leaders are very familiar with the phenomenon of synergy, particularly in the context of mergers and acquisitions. It is commonplace for executives to seek the benefits of market, product, and revenue synergies with potential merger or acquisition candidates and even to continually evaluate synergy opportunities across divisions of their own companies, looking for greater benefits. The benefits achieved when curiosity and courage are combined are an exponential impact that I call the C^2 Factor.

It was 2008, Lehman Brothers had collapsed, and the country was facing a financial crisis. Nani Coloretti's job as the budget director for the San Francisco Mayor required big doses of the C^2 Factor. Coloretti, now a senior vice president at the Urban Institute, told me:

> We needed to cut big parts of our budget and try to find ways to lever-age more revenue at the same time. We were cutting services, jobs, people's livelihood, and community-based organizations' budgets. There was no good news. But we had a series of community hearings to explain the actions. They were terrible meetings. Some people seemed to come to the hearings just to yell at me.

> I had to do an internal shift and remind myself that all the anger, fear, and unhappiness was not directed at me personally. It was directed at the situation and possibly the mayor, but it was not directed at me. That created the mind space for me to be very curious and try to understand what people were saying. And what I was most curious about was what was underneath what they were saying. I wanted to find out what they really wanted out of this process and to understand if there was a way to find solutions that would help meet some of the needs of the most people. I used all kinds of curiosity and courage to do those things, both to stand up for my staff and to model courage and curiosity in very tense settings, hopefully teaching it at the same time to my staff.

This is champion leadership at its essence – engaging the C^2 Factor to solve a complex problem not only for one's organizations, but also for the world.

When curiosity and courage are used synergistically, we can achieve profound results, often with impacts rippling far beyond what we may have imagined. So how do they work together? We often need courage to be curious and curiosity helps us be brave. The term C^2 Factor refers exactly to this powerful relationship. In my decades as an executive coach and from interviews with accomplished executives, I have found this factor to be the cornerstone of the personalities of champion leaders. It enables them to capitalize on the rapid changes in our world. Relying on only one of these qualities results in suboptimal performance.

Examining how curiosity and courage are related helps us see how they contribute to champion leadership. Seeing what happens when they are not present together can serve as a warning of what to watch out for and illustrate who we do or do not want to emulate.

YOU GOTTA HAVE COURAGE TO BE CURIOUS

1. Admitting You Don't Know

It requires courage for leaders to acknowledge that they don't know something and are genuinely curious about the answer. Nani Coloretti had to call upon just that type of courage when she was appointed Deputy Secretary of the U.S. Department of Housing and Urban Development (HUD):

> HUD was operationally weak at the time and people thought of me as an effective leader. However, I did not have a substantive expertise in the housing portfolio, which is quite complex, and the agency itself is very complex. It's a very complicated, mission-driven place. So that was an area where I had to draw upon curiosity and courage, just to figure out my approach to the job.
>
> I had been a career Federal employee so I understood that when I was parachuted into that job, people were wondering what I was doing there and whether they could trust me or if they had to listen to me. I knew that I was in over my head and didn't really understand any of the portfolios or what they had been doing for the last two to three decades. And, I knew I was going to have to facilitate complicated issues and bring them to resolution.
>
> So, I used courage to be vulnerable and admit that I was not the expert and that I didn't know the issues, and I used curiosity to learn from them. I met with every single senior manager in federal space, 80 members of the SES (Senior Executive Service). I expressed curiosity about what they're doing, what they liked most about their job and what they wished they could change with a magic wand.

Evidently, courage and curiosity are working synergistically here.

And it takes even more courage to scrutinize what we think we know. "We need to be most curious about the things we know for sure," Anil Lewis, the Executive Director of Blindness Initiatives, National Federation of the Blind, told me. Marshall Goldsmith, the preeminent executive coach and author of *What Got You Here Won't Get You There*, warns against the tendency of leaders to want to be the smartest person in the room. It is not easy to surrender one's expertise and be curious. Most leaders get promoted by having answers, not questions.

Figure 2.1 shows how courage is often necessary for us to be curious.

Pause for a moment and think about sitting with a group of peers or the team you lead and imagine telling them that you don't completely understand what they are talking about. Feel easy? It doesn't to me. Or, what about asking for their opinion about how you might improve your leadership and insisting that they need to come up with one suggestion. Are you curious about their opinions or are you sure you know what they think? It takes tremendous courage to challenge our very strong brains to be less certain and more curious.

FIGURE 2.1
When courage helps us be curious.

2. Encountering Unpleasant Discoveries

If we ask questions and are truly curious, we run the risk of making unpleasant discoveries. It requires the fortitude to have honest conversations. "A big part of leadership is really listening with curiosity, with respect, with courage. What you learn may not be comfortable because while we've done some good, we can always do better," said Summer Stephan, a nationally recognized leader for a wide variety of initiatives ranging from human trafficking to treatment of veterans. Summer is District Attorney of the second largest DA's office in California, the fifth largest in the country with about a thousand employees.

She further said:

> I hear a lot of leaders say they want to invite ideas, but they don't really because they don't want to hear that they haven't been doing it correctly. They don't have the courage to listen. And it makes others give up if they aren't grounded in courage. Instead of continuing to ask the hard questions they just give up on their ideas.

- What questions are you afraid to ask?
- What answers do you reject because they challenge your assumptions?
- When was the last time you asked your team to play "devil's advocate" about an idea you feel passionate about?

We need courage to be curious about leadership. Happily, if we are curious, it is easier to be brave.

———

IT HELPS TO BE CURIOUS IF YOU WANT TO BE BRAVE

1. Curiosity Is the Bravery Elixir

First, a little psychoneurology about what happens in our brains when we feel threatened. When we sense danger of any kind, a very primitive part of our brain called the amygdala gets activated. The amygdala reacts to stimuli in "all or none" terms. Its sole motivation is to get us to safety, but it is a terrible problem-solver because it thinks in black and white terms. This part of the brain has served us well through our evolution as a survival mechanism; but for leaders, parents, spouses, and friends, it can be problematic.

Because amygdala thinking generally sees few options and usually defaults to negatives, it shuts down conversation, creates hostility, and keeps us stuck in conflict. Curiosity is the elixir that changes our fear-based defenses into true courage. If we can engage our curiosity, it will move us out of the amygdala and into the forebrain – the master problem-solver!

In a moment of crisis, it is usually necessary to change our physiology as an initial step to competently cope with the situation. We need to take a deep breath (or a few) to help us calm down. But if the brain keeps feeding the amygdala with danger warnings, we will be right back where we started. That's when curiosity is our ally. When we use our curiosity to ask questions, our understanding deepens, nuances are noticed, complexities emerge, and we begin to see options and opportunities (Figure 2.2).

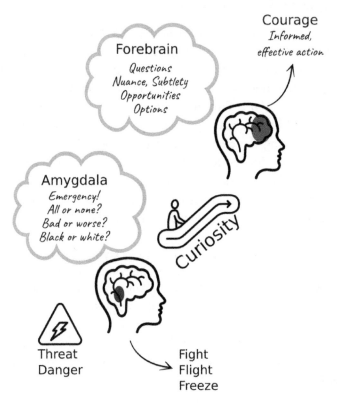

FIGURE 2.2
How curiosity evokes courage.

"Probably my most courageous move was when I left a very comfortable, wonderful role as a senior vice president running government affairs, to build a business with hundreds of engineers," said former Cisco executive Laura Ipsen. The now CEO of Ellucian said:

> I left all of the safety nets, left my office across from the CEO to move to an engineering building. I had gotten very curious about how to use technology around sustainability, to deliver new capabilities to the electric grid.
>
> I feel like you become more courageous because you're just really fascinated and curious. It propelled me forward. I learned ahead of the curve. I left the government fears and built a whole team. I feel like you become more courageous because you're just really fascinated and curious. It propelled me forward. I learned ahead of the curve. I left the government fears and built a whole team.

2. Using Curiosity to Persevere

Curiosity helps fuel our courage to make decisions that impact our careers and our organizations. It fuels our courage to persevere in the face of opposition.

In her journey to build a special victims' unit that has been compared favorably to the one seen on the television show *Law and Order, Special Victims Unit,* Summer Stephan tackled child trafficking, prostitution, addiction, and violence. Instead of simply applying more force implementing the current treatment approaches as a means to be more effective, she looked for the root causes behind the problems. She questioned whether the then current treatment approaches were actually working. The answers fueled her courage to try new ways to address the problems. She faced many challenges along the way.

> There were points and junctures where I was trying to figure out if all of the no's, failures, and rejections meant that I was on the wrong path. In those pivotal moments, I asked myself "Am I missing something? Is this not really a problem? Why is there so much resistance to these new ideas?"

Summer's search for answers fueled her courage to make real changes. Her curiosity and courage are what led to the development of the nationally renowned Special Victims Unit.

The next time you are in a situation that feels threatening, whether it's interpersonal or something happening in the marketplace, geopolitics, or the natural environment, you can calm your amygdala with a breath, and consciously invite your curiosity. Get out of flight, fight, or freeze by asking questions like the following:

- What is actually happening?
- What assumptions am I making?
- What things can I control?
- How many options are here?
- What is the next first action I need to take?

Engage your curiosity. It will help you be brave.

THE C² FACTOR

We know that curiosity and courage are separate human motivations and, indeed, some leaders have more of one than the other. In the following section, I will show you more about what happens when that occurs. What I discovered in my interviews is that for champion leaders, curiosity and courage frequently exist close together, are mutually beneficial, and potentiate each other. This symbiosis and synergy is the C² Factor.

How can we tell whether we have the C² Factor? What happens to our leadership if we only have one component and not the other? What are some examples of leaders who use the C² Factor to accomplish remarkable goals? And who are some of the leaders who appear to lack the C² Factor?

The infinity symbol in Figure 2.3 represents the alchemy of curiosity and courage found in the C² Factor. It takes courage to be curious and curiosity helps you be courageous. They interact and potentiate each other.

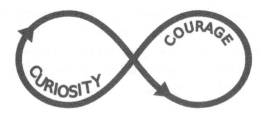

FIGURE 2.3
The alchemy of curiosity and courage.

So, what happens if you have neither of these qualities or one without the other? Figure 2.4 illustrates the results. We can look at them one at a time.

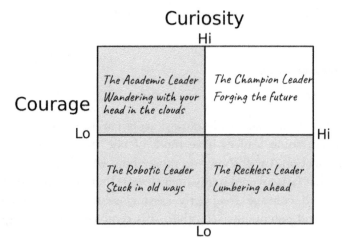

FIGURE 2.4
The C² leader diagnostic quadrant.

LACKING THE C² FACTOR

1. The Robotic Leader: Neither Curious nor Courageous

If you are low on both courage and curiosity, you are simply stuck doing the same things over and over, like a robot, and are likely to become obsolete!

During the global financial crisis of 2007–2008, it became apparent that General Motors (GM) was being led by robotic leaders.[1] GM leadership refused to transform their product line and as one executive who was in middle management at the time told me, "They simply tried harder to do what they'd always done." Their North American performance plummeted, and they dropped from 50% to 15% market share. They clearly lacked the courage and curiosity to understand the changing market and explore new opportunities. Had it not been for the automotive bailout money provided by the government and a change in leadership, they would have surely met their demise.

Robotic leadership is not limited to manufacturing, however. It can be found in any industry sector. Financial services can have robotic leadership. A parliamentary report released in December 2020 in Great Britain[2] revealed that 50 billion pounds (about $67 billion) of paper money was "missing" from the country's cash supply. In addition, the report noted that the Bank of England "seemed to lack curiosity" about where it had gone. Since that report, there has been no indication of attempts to investigate. It seems obvious that not only did the Bank of England lack curiosity, but there was a lack of courageous leadership as well.

Nor is the telecommunication/information technology industry immune. Nokia is another example of a company that suffered from robotic leadership. When other mobile companies started understanding how data, not voice, was the future of communication, Nokia kept focusing on hardware because the management feared alienating users if they changed too much. Other examples of well-known companies that suffered from robotic leadership include Sears, Palm, Blackberry, Blockbuster, Toys R Us, Tower Records, and Kodak.

The robotic leader is stuck in the mud trying to plow ahead in the same old way.

2. The Academic Leader: Lots of Curiosity, Little Courage

If you have a lot of curiosity but no courage, you will not be able to make use of your discoveries to improve either your life or your business. You'll wander with wonder perhaps, but aimlessly and ineffectively. This is academic leadership. Often innately curious, scientists, engineers, researchers, and many other professionals make meaningful contributions to our society and play valuable roles in most organizations because of their curiosity. However, when they become leaders, they need to embrace courage, or they risk becoming academic leaders.

Several executives at high-tech firms commented to me that engineers by nature are very curious, but are not incentivized to take risks. "Engineers are rewarded for output but not outcome," speculated former Google executive Jennifer Lin, who is now SVP/CPO of Trimble. In other words, their job is not about executing the results in the marketplace. Elizabeth Eby, currently the CFO at NeoPhotonics, and a strong believer in the power of curiosity, told me about a lawyer she once worked with who needed the courage to take action:

> She was an exceptionally good lawyer, endlessly curious about every aspect of the business and every aspect of the contract. So much so that a number of times we had to turn to her and say, "you need to get the contract done. I love your curiosity, but you need to get the contract done."

Healthcare companies, hospitals, research institutes, colleges, and universities often suffer because executives are selected based on their professional expertise, not their leadership capabilities. This is not to suggest that doctors, scientists, engineers, or other professionals cannot be champion leaders. They can, but they must not assume they are automatically suited for the job. Other nonspecialists can also suffer from paralysis by analysis or become enamored with some new technology such that their leadership is academic and a detriment to their organizations. Leaders who are curious also need to embrace courage – careful assessment of risk and taking action to achieve a worthy goal.

To become a champion leader, the academic needs the courage to execute.

3. The Reckless Leader: All Courage, No Curiosity

If all you have is courage with no curiosity, you will miss important information that is necessary to take judicious action. You will act, but your risk assessment will likely be inadequate because you have not inquired enough into the situation. Without curiosity, reckless leaders fail to consider the opinions of others or to ask questions to discover obstacles and opportunities. Without curiosity, questions can be used merely to confirm the leader's evaluation of the situation. A reckless leader lumbers through the environment often leaving havoc in his path.

Examples of reckless leaders abound. In world politics, North Korea's Kim Jong-un and Brazilian President Jair Bolsonaro who refused to acknowledge the seriousness of the coronavirus crisis are two such examples. Business headlines are full of scandals in which leaders of formerly well-respected companies plunged ahead with no apparent reflection or inquisitiveness. The lack of curiosity is so astounding that it seems leaders are purposely refusing to look thoroughly at a situation before taking action.

- When Volkswagen's vehicles were found to have cheated U.S. emissions tests, CEO Martin Winterkorn[3] claimed to have no knowledge of wrongdoing. Nor did he display significant curiosity in understanding how events took place or how to prevent them in the future.
- Similarly, the leaders at Boeing claimed to have no awareness that there were problems with the design of the 737 max plane's navigation system.[4]
- Jean-Sébastien Jacques was the CEO of Rio Tinto, an Anglo-Australian multinational mining corporation, when the company destroyed a 46,000-year-old sacred Indigenous site in Australia in order to expand an iron ore mine. He was apparently unaware and not curious about the value of those sites.[5]
- When interviewed after the U.S. Office of the Comptroller of the Currency found risk management deficiencies that "constituted reckless, unsafe or unsound practices," leading to improper charges to hundreds of thousands of consumers, Wells Fargo CEO, Tom Sloan, declared that he, his board, and all of his 260,000 employees thought he was doing a great job.[6]

These leaders seem to value expediency and short-term gain over thoughtful inquiry into how these actions will reflect on the company's brand and ultimately its success. They are willing to be "courageous" and take action or sometimes refuse to take action despite pressure from multiple stakeholders.

Reckless leaders are often in error, but never in doubt. They have the will to take action, but lack the curiosity that will keep them in touch with the results of their actions.

THE CHAMPION LEADER: CURIOUS AND COURAGEOUS

It takes both curiosity and courage to be a champion leader – one who forges the future by gathering information from disparate sources and taking action even in the face of ambiguity. The champion leader dares to try, learns from feedback, and course corrects to create the future. Jackie Sturm is the epitome of such a leader.

1. Tackling Terror in the Supply Chain

Jackie Sturm, Corporate Vice President of Global Supply Chain Operations at Intel, told me: "I learned a couple of maxims early in my career, but one of the most important ones is that you cannot rely on others to ask you to play. You need to step up and really push yourself into spaces where you can be impactful. Leaders are really here to try to identify what's going on in the world and figure out how to forge a new path that supports the growth or the success of an organization. To do that, they need to be looking at the world from a different perspective. They need to be sensing and learning from what's happening around them and that requires a lot of curiosity."

Sturm told me several stories from her storied Silicon Valley career path from Hewlett Packard to Apple to Intel that demonstrate how she applies her C² Factor, but one that seemed particularly powerful was about Intel's curtailment of the use of "conflict minerals."

> One of the areas that we are responsible for in my organization is what's called supply chain sustainability, and a key aspect of that is human rights. Back in 2009 my organization and I were informed about what was called "conflict minerals." Armed insurgents in Africa were exploiting and terrorizing the civilian artisanal mining population and stealing the profits.
>
> These insurgents were able to commit severe atrocities because they could take the profits from the mining work that these people did and fund their continued terrorism activities in the local area. The people on my team were crushed by the idea of what was happening to these local people – the raping of women, killing children, and enslaving the men. They wanted to do something.
>
> With the then CEO, I decided we had to make an impact and bring about change. But we'd never been to Africa; nobody on our team had ever been

to Africa. We had never talked to a miner. I couldn't pick out tantalum or tungsten or tin if you put them all in front of me. We decided we should go to Africa and talk to miners and see the mines. We enlisted the state department and some local governments in Africa and said, "Take us on a tour; let us see what the mines are. Let us figure out how the money flows and the root cause."

So we traveled a quarter of a million miles in the first year to Africa, and up to Mongolia too, to better understand the flow of what happens to this material, and then we designed a "bag and tag" chain of custody that allowed us to let the compliant material flow to the smelter, which was the last point at which you could differentiate the material. Our vendors, the smelters, would only accept the compliant material and reject minerals sourced from the insurgents.

This change eventually created an economic embargo. In the first year we implemented the bag and tag system, it took a significant amount of illicit profit out of one mineral. So, in 2012, we made a public commitment that by the end of that year, there would be no conflict tantalum in any Intel microprocessor. It took us four years to get there but we were able to do it. Then we said by the end of 2013 we would address the other three minerals. We achieved that goal by mid-February 2012.

All this positive change came from being curious, asking "how does this work? What is the root cause? How do we step into the breach with a public commitment and people on the ground?"

Listening to this, I had to add, "And it also came from courage – the courage to be public, the courage to go to Africa, the courage to take on the status quo, the courage to disrupt the supply chain of essential materials."

Today, Jackie and Intel are curious on how to grow this even further; a key technology initiative for their 2030 RISE strategy is to significantly expand the impact in responsible minerals and accelerate the creation of new sourcing standards.

Leaders with the C^2 Factor – what a difference from the other leadership types!

2. Postscript: The C^2 Factor Does Not Stand Alone

Leaders with the C^2 Factor stand out as champions, particularly suited for today. This is not to suggest that these are the only qualities needed to lead successfully. Leaders must also have vision and passion and be able to communicate in a way that inspires others. They need to be accountable and competent, but it is their C² Factor that differentiates them from the rest.

There may be times when it is necessary to call upon more of one aspect of the C² Factor than the other. At any given time, a leader may be on different points along the infinity curve, but with the C² Factor, there is a constant oscillation between curiosity and courage. Curiosity keeps us alert in our environment, looking beneath the surface and asking "what?" and "why?" Courage enables us to engage, to take action in the face of some ambiguity about the outcome. Curiosity will keep our courage on course as we adjust and respond to changing conditions or new information. It provides the fuel for the consideration necessary for true courage. Courage then propels us to take action again.

The C² Factor enables us to effectively navigate decisions and challenges today and equips us to anticipate the future and respond to its surprises. It makes us champions – quick learners, nimble, able to act, fall down sometimes, but when we do, get up and move ahead.

3. Where Are You and Where Do You Want to Go?

Take the Champion Leader Diagnostic located on the website below and compare yourself with some of the leaders described above to benchmark yourself and your leadership.

Visit the website: www.CourageousCuriousLeaders.com

We can apply the C² Factor to ourselves, our relationships, our teams and organizations, and the world. Doing so will improve business outcomes and the quality of life for ourselves and the people around us.

NOTES

1. DeBord, Matthew. "How GM Went from a Government Bailout and Bankruptcy to Being One of the World's Best-Run Car Companies a Decade Later." *Business Insider*, October 20, 2018. https://www.businessinsider.com/gm-mary-barra-management-helped-save-automaker-2018-10.
2. Schaverien, Anna. "Bank of England Rebuked Over 'Missing' $67 Billion of Cash." *The New York Times*, December 04, 2020. www.nytimes.com/2020/12/04/world/europee/bank-england-missing-cash.html.
3. Ewing, Jack. "Martin Winterkorn, Ex-C.E.O. of Volkswagen, Is under Investigation." *The New York Times*, June 20, 2016. https://www.nytimes.com/2016/06/21/business/international/volkswagen-winterkorn-germany.html.

4. Chokshi, Niraj. "House Condemns Boeing and F.A.A. in 737 Max Disasters." *The New York Times*. September 16, 2020. https://www.nytimes.com/2020/09/16/business/boeing-737-max-house-report.html.

5. Reuters Staff. "Rio Tinto's Sacred Indigenous Caves Blast Scandal." *Reuters Business News*, March 03, 2021. https://www.reuters.com/article/us-australia-mining-indigenous/rio-tintos-sacred-indigenous-caves-blast-scandal-idUSKCN2AV0OU.

6. Merle, Renae. "Warren to Wells Fargo CEO: 'You Should Be Fired'." *The Washington Post*, October 03, 2017. https://www.washingtonpost.com/news/business/wp/2017/10/03/ceo-to-congress-wells-fargo-is-better-bank-today-than-it-was-a-year-ago.

3

The C² Factor Begins at Home: Start with You

Inner calm. Clarity of thought. Confidence in action. Now more than ever these themes are necessary if we are to make sense of the surrounding chaos, be sure-footed among ambiguity, and be at ease in the pressure cooker that is leadership. Champion leaders know the path to this centered state of being starts deep within themselves and use mindfulness as a tool to achieve equanimity, invite curiosity about themselves, and find perspective on external events. Mindfulness is the ultimate form of curiosity and the self-awareness it brings breeds the courage required to confront hidden biases and leadership hubris. With mindfulness, champion leaders reap the benefits of not only becoming more effective, but also of living a more fulfilling life.

> I've been up since 5:00 a.m., been to the gym, grabbed a green smoothie on my way to the office, met with my team on Zoom, and am about to go to the leadership team meeting where I'm presenting the deal I hope will be approved for the next step. I've got meetings with the CEOs at three start-ups, need to connect with the strategic venture capital division of X (an overseas manufacturing firm,) and I am trying to hire a new Ph.D. for the R&D team that is in Singapore.

This is how the 8:00 a.m. coaching session began with my client, a senior executive at a venture capital firm in the Washington, DC, area.

So many of the executives I've worked with come to me tethered to a completely full calendar, with back-to-back corporate meetings from early morning until well into the evening. Board members, shareholders, key

DOI: 10.4324/9781003212881-3

customers, and community groups all want their time and attention – as do their families. Leading in today's digitally connected world where social, cultural, political, and economic events ripple across the globe, they are expected to continually perform at the highest levels. They must navigate often ambiguous and fast-changing circumstances that profoundly impact market conditions, require rethinking business models, redesigning organizational structure, and adopting agile management practices.

As leaders, the repercussions of our decisions cascade down through our organizations, impacting every aspect of the company. The leader is the role model establishing the corporate culture, the navigator charting the company's course, and the standard by which performance is gauged. The weight of these responsibilities can be daunting. And what about the quality of your life? More and more we are recognizing that work and life do not need to be a zero-sum game and, in fact, executives with richer lives are better leaders. Not to mention, you deserve it!

This is when engaging our C² Factor is essential. We need to draw on our courage to make ourselves pause and have curiosity – about what is going on inside us and in our immediate environment. It is from this internal platform that we can take effective action. Mindfulness is a special kind of applied curiosity that enables and enhances the courage inherent in agile leadership.

GAZING AT OUR NAVELS WITH THE C² FACTOR

The benefits of meditation and mindfulness have been documented for some time now. Research confirms that mindfulness meditation increases working memory, improves focus and attention, reduces rumination and anxiety, expands creativity, and enhances emotional intelligence. The list of well-known CEOs, champion leaders, who espouse mindfulness as central to their success and who regularly meditate[1] is longer than we have time for here.

The list includes the following:

- Ariana Huffington of the Huffington Post who says, "I wish I'd appreciated (earlier) just how powerful it can be to introduce just five minutes of meditation to your day."

- Ray Dalio, founder of Bridgewater Associates, the world's largest hedge fund who built many meditation principles into his firm's culture, who says, "Meditation more than anything in my life was the biggest ingredient of whatever success I've had."
- Marc Benioff of Salesforce, who says: "I enjoy meditation, which I've been doing for over a decade – probably to help relieve the stress I was going through when I was working at Oracle."
- Roger Berkowitz, CEO of Legal Sea Foods, who says: "The first thing I do in the morning is retreat to my den and meditate … I meditate twice a day for 20 minutes. Sometimes, I'm wrestling with an issue before meditation, and afterward the answer is suddenly clear."
- Bob Stiller founder, former chairman of Green Mountain Coffee, who says: "If you have a meditation practice, you can be much more effective in meetings. Meditation helps develop your abilities to focus better and to accomplish your tasks."
- Bill Gates, founder of Microsoft, who says: "Meditation is simply exercise for the mind."

If there was a drug that could enhance our well-being at work and home to the degree that regular practice of what mindfulness meditation produces, people would line up around the block for hours to purchase such a drug.

And yet, it seems to be hard for us to establish this habit. This free, readily available, simple practice that is appropriate for everyone seems too hard for us to do. Why? It's the same thing that makes it hard to get to the gym every day. It's the same thing that makes it hard to eat a salad instead of French fries. It's hard to do what we know is best for us. We need to call upon our C² Factor.

To have mindfulness meditation a part of our daily routine requires engaging our C² Factor in several ways. We need the courage to stop doing and sit! Sitting without reading or listening to a podcast, news report, or music – doing nothing – can feel like a waste of time. It takes determination to power through these initial reactions. And it takes courage to approach this process with curiosity and to focus the spotlight on ourselves.

1. Meditation, Mindfulness, and the Courage to be Bored

Mindfulness is simply paying attention to the here and now of our experience, noticing what we are taking in through our senses (hearing, seeing, touching, and even tasting and smelling) as well as our thoughts and feelings as they arise. Mindfulness is observing our moment-to-moment experience – both inner and outer, in an accepting way without judgment.

Meditation is a method for developing and improving our ability to be mindful in our daily lives. When we meditate, we set aside a period of time to focus on making these observations and nothing else! That is the challenge. That requires courage. Then we bring our curiosity.

We sit and breathe and notice. I am usually able to do this for about a nanosecond before my mind begins to wander. I am making lists, planning what to do next, ruminating on something from the past, getting annoyed by the noise from the lawn mower outside … You get the picture. As it turns out, that is OK. It's the nature of our brains. As soon as we notice that we have been captured by one of these, we engage our curiosity and simply notice what is going on. Then we bring our focus back to our breath. It is this bringing back of our focus that creates the new neural pathways necessary for mindfulness. In fact, mindfulness has been shown to physically change several regions of the brain in as little as eight weeks.[2]

Mindfulness is the antidote for a wandering mind. Mindfulness improves our capacity for focused attention. It helps us prevent ourselves from running from one activity to the next and constantly trying to head down different paths simultaneously. In addition, by becoming an observer of our own thinking process, our field of conscious awareness is expanded and more options become available – more possibilities of ways to respond.

When we apply curiosity to what our brain is thinking about and what it is doing with the thoughts, feelings, and urges it's producing, we begin to realize that these are just productions of our minds, not a replication of reality.[3] Although ultimately a liberating realization, it takes courage to accept this. Our brains are very powerful and protest against this idea. One way I help my clients understand this is by asking them to think of a lemon. When we think of a lemon, it is easy to see the lemon, to smell a lemon, and almost taste the lemon, but we are very clear that there is no lemon present. The problem is that our minds treat our thoughts as if the lemon was really there.

Mindfulness allows us to recognize that thoughts are just thoughts, beliefs, stories that may be very useful, but are only interpretations of reality, not reality itself. This means that there are many more ways to understand what is happening than our brain is telling us. But our brains fight this idea. The metaphor that captures this for me is "your mind is the jailer holding captive a prisoner, but your mind is the prisoner." To challenge the power of our minds, now that takes some C² Factor!

The next time you have 15 unscheduled minutes, instead of checking email or making a call, have the courage to close your eyes and just sit. Breathe deeply and let your mind go wherever it wants. Just notice your thoughts. Be curious about your thoughts but try not to get absorbed in them. Let your thoughts slip in and out of your mind. Breathe deeply. When you open your eyes, you will approach your world from a more stable, centered place.

2. Feelings? What Feelings?

When we are mindful, we become aware of our feelings as well as our thoughts. Activity can keep us unaware of feelings we don't like – insecurities, doubts, frustration, fear. Not only are these emotions uncomfortable, but they are also frankly unacceptable in the business arena. American optimism and confidence are praised and admired. These other feelings, not so much. Early in my career I remember asking the director of an organization where I had been hired as a consultant, what his feelings were about the sudden departure of a key member of his staff, to which he replied "I'm an adult. I don't have feelings."

But being unaware of unpleasant feelings does not make them go away. Driven out of consciousness, these feelings act on us instead of for us. If we are unaware of feeling threatened, for example, we will not take the measures necessary to explore where the threat might be coming from (is it the result of some personal history or is it a warning of real impending danger). Instead, we may instinctively fight or freeze and inadequately deal with the situation.

Becoming aware of our feelings helps us to experience them without those feelings flipping us into over- or underreaction. Neuroscience tells us, "if you name it, you tame it." Just as we recognize that thoughts are just thoughts, we can recognize that we are not one and the same as our feelings. Notice the difference in your experience when you say, "I am anxious" versus, when you say, "I am having the feeling of anxiety." Better still, how does it affect your experience when you say, "I notice that I am having the feeling of anxiety?"

If we apply the C² Factor and have the courage to be curious about our feelings, we become aware that feelings come and go. Feelings are like clouds in the sky. They are sometimes large, sometimes small, sometimes ominous, sometimes fluffy, but they always come and go. They are in the sky; they are not the same as the sky. You are the sky. There is an impermanence to our experience and whatever it is, "this too shall pass."

When we realize we are not our feelings, that there is more to us than the particular feeling we are having at the moment, there is a certain liberation from those feelings. We are free from their dictatorship that can get in the way of us being the best version of ourselves both professionally and in our private lives.

Once we become aware of our thoughts and feelings, we can begin to see patterns in our responses and because we engage the C² Factor, see more options as to how to react. Attunement to our feelings helps us stay present and engaged. This self-awareness and perhaps, paradoxically, acceptance results in positive and often permanent changes in our thinking patterns and physical responses. And because we are truly in charge of how we respond, we develop greater confidence and build the kind of life we want.

Pay attention to your feelings, especially when you are stressed. For example, notice if there is a pattern to how you feel under pressure. Perhaps you need to know details and be in control. Or perhaps you feel tired and need reassurance from those around you. Perhaps you become unusually enthusiastic and optimistic about charging into the future. Are your responses consistent regardless of the situation? If so, these are patterned responses. When you are aware of your patterns, you may consciously open yourself to a vast array of alternative responses.

3. Using the Beginner's Mind and Embracing Ambiguity

Before I was an executive coach and consultant, I was a very competent psychotherapist with a thriving private practice and working with highly accomplished clients in the Washington, DC, area. I was used to thinking of myself as very good at what I did. I was confident and successful. So, it was very uncomfortable for me to go into a field where I was a novice. Fortunately, I have enough of the C² Factor that I was really curious about how consulting worked and had the courage to allow myself to feel incompetent.

There are benefits of moving from one domain to another because we bring to the new domain a beginner's mind. We question how things are done, not merely to challenge them, but to truly understand.

"The beginner's mind" is a phrase borrowed from Zen Buddhism, meaning having an attitude of openness, eagerness, and lack of preconceptions when studying a subject just as a beginner would. In other words, having an attitude of profound curiosity. When we move from one domain into another or are in unfamiliar circumstances, this attitude arises easily, but it is difficult for leaders who come to business challenges with lots of prior experience and accompanying assumptions about how to approach challenges.

It takes enormous courage to adopt an attitude of not knowing, but that is exactly what leaders need in order to navigate through the disruption many of us face now and most of us are likely to face sometime in the future. According to a 2018 article in the *McKinsey Quarterly*,[4] what is required of leaders is a kind of inner agility, centered leadership that is "comfortable with not knowing."

The essential skill and mindset necessary for agile organizations is centered leadership that is comfortable with not knowing. To spot opportunities – and threats – in this environment, we must teach ourselves how to have a more comfortable and creative relationship with uncertainty. That means learning how to relax at the edge of uncertainty, paying attention to subtle clues both in our environment and in how we experience the moment that may inform unconventional action.

McKinsey's advice for leaders:

> Embrace your ignorance. Good new ideas can come from anywhere, competitors can emerge from neighboring industries, and a single technology product can reshape your business. In such a world, listening – and thinking – from a place of not knowing is a critical means of encouraging the discovery of original, unexpected, breakthrough ideas.

To adopt this beginner's mind, we need to be able to approach our minds with curiosity and have the courage to challenge what we might find there. Using the C² Factor, we can explore the assumptions we bring to situations and notice how they can limit what we see as options and opportunities.

SHINING THE C² FACTOR BEYOND
THE END OF YOUR NOSE

Figure 3.1 maps our knowledge and our awareness of our knowledge. The upper right quadrant is the result of education and other learning experiences. In the previous section, we challenged staying only in upper left quadrant, but it certainly has its place in champion leadership. Quadrant C is important to address but that is for another day.

What we are concerned about in this section is the lower left quadrant – the "unknown unknowns," as Donald Rumsfeld once described the most interesting part of security reports.[5] When we engage the C² Factor for our individual development, we cultivate mindfulness, a tolerance for difficult feelings, and a comfort with ambiguity. Because we recognize that we are separate from our thoughts, we can observe their content. What are the things that we don't know but don't realize we don't know?

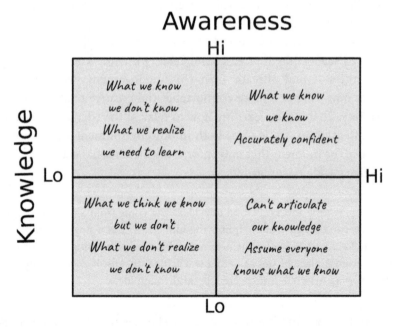

FIGURE 3.1
Window of awareness.

1. Heuristics and Cognitive Biases

Think about the last time you drove to visit a friend or a relative. You got in the car and began driving at the appropriate speed. This decision was not based on a deliberate calculation, but rather your sense of what was safe and well-suited to the situation.

When we drive, we do not have to consciously ask ourselves to assess the road conditions, the weather, how tired or rested we feel, whether time is of the essence, the chances of getting a speeding ticket, etc. We do not apply analysis based on the physics of the tires on the road, the aerodynamics of our car, or the wind velocity. We automatically choose a speed based on our internal sense of what is safe (regardless of the posted speed limit) and drive. That is a heuristic.

A heuristic is a mental shortcut that allows us to solve problems and make decisions quickly without extensive deliberation. They are rule-of-thumb strategies that shorten decision-making time and help us avoid "analysis paralysis." Heuristics help us get through the day without having to constantly stop to think about our next course of action.

Our mental models of how things work help us decide what time to get up in the morning, how much to eat for lunch, how to quickly find facts about a subject we might be interested in (notice the automatic tendency to go to the internet to use Google).

In conditions of uncertainty, professionals use "fast-and-frugal heuristics" to make quick decisions using a single cue or a recognizable pattern of cues. Whenever we make an "educated guess," we are using a heuristic. We are taking what we have learned and applying it without having to consciously decide how to do so.

Heuristics are helpful in many situations, but they can also lead to cognitive biases. The following are among the most common cognitive biases.

Availability: This involves judging the likelihood of an event happening and making decisions based upon how easy it is to bring something to mind. We tend to assume that events are more common if we can quickly remember them. One of the most common is the assumption that flying is more dangerous than driving because plane crashes come to mind so much more quickly than car accidents.

The underestimation of the risk of investing in new mobile app IPOs is another example because it is so easy to remember the enormous success of companies like Airbnb, Instagram, Uber, LinkedIn, and WhatsApp. Yet the vast majority of these ventures do not survive.

Source confusion: We often forget where we got information, so we are unable to distinguish things that really happened from things we overheard at an airport, saw on a TV show, or even dreamed!

Imagine your leadership team is discussing possible new technologies to invest in. Lots of ideas are being thrown around – artificial intelligence, robotic process automation, quantum computing, nanotechnology, virtual reality, blockchain, etc. During the brainstorm, you have an extremely negative reaction to the idea of nanotechnology because of the dangers and inherent risks it presents. Unfortunately, unbeknownst to you, that information came to you when you overheard a conversation at a cocktail party.

Confirmation bias: This is the very common tendency to find or interpret information that confirms our beliefs and minimizes or discredits information that does not support them. This is so ubiquitous that I hardly know what example to use. My own are not so obvious to me, so I will choose one that results in a decision that I think makes no sense.

Despite the fact that the COVID virus has run rampant across the globe wreaking havoc in its path – severe symptoms and death for some, long-term residual effects for others, an economy rattled, and a healthcare system seriously challenged – some people have refused to get vaccinated against it. This can only be explained by confirmation bias.

Having decided that they are not going to get vaccinated, they find all the facts that validate the decision as reasonable. They find facts that indicate that the vaccine is not safe, pointing to reports of one of them seeming to cause strokes in young women and of people who had allergic reactions to the injection. They find facts that confirm the vaccines are not necessary – that many people never caught the virus or had very mild symptoms if they did. I am sure there are more. The evidence that vaccines are necessary to protect ourselves and others is dismissed or ignored.

Motivated bias: When we have put a great deal of effort into something or invested time and money in an undertaking and then discover that it has some major flaws, we resist changing course. Motivated bias causes us to fail to recognize shortcomings and inherent risks and forge ahead. We throw good money after bad. I've seen this several times with the implementation of new software when, in the middle of the project, it becomes clear that the software is not suitable for the organization's requirements. The company has invested so much money that they find ways to "massage" it so that it appears to be a good solution.

A number of years ago, I had a client who was a brilliant software designer. He complained to me about his new manager, who clearly had motivated bias in the kind of changes she asked my client to make. "She keeps asking me to paint the building when the foundation is unstable!"

Present bias: This occurs when we overvalue short-term gains and ignore long-term aims, gains, and consequences – selling a substandard product or service because of its large profit margin while ignoring its impact on the company's brand and repute, for example.

What makes these biases so dangerous is not their existence; they are natural mental models. The danger is when they occur without the use of our C² Factor which invites us to be curious about them and have the courage to challenge their applicability.

As social psychologist David Dunning[6] in a 2017 article for the *Pacific Standard* aptly put it:

> An ignorant mind is precisely not a spotless, empty vessel, but one that's filled with the clutter of irrelevant or misleading life experiences, theories, facts, intuitions, strategies, algorithms, heuristics, metaphors, and hunches that regrettably have the look and feel of useful and accurate knowledge. This clutter is an unfortunate by-product of one of our greatest strengths as a species.
>
> We are unbridled pattern recognizers and profligate theorizers. Often, our theories are good enough to get us through the day, or at least to an age when we can procreate. But our genius for creative storytelling, combined with our inability to detect our own ignorance, can sometimes lead to situations that are embarrassing, unfortunate, or downright dangerous … As the humorist Josh Billings once put it, "It ain't what you don't know that gets you into trouble. It's what you know for sure that just ain't so."
>
> Ironically, one thing many people "know" about this quote is that it was first uttered by Mark Twain or Will Rogers – which just ain't so.

2. Fighting the Dunning–Kruger[7] Effect

Speaking of David Dunning, perhaps one of the most pernicious biases we can be subject to without a strong C² Factor is the so-called Dunning–Kruger effect. In 1999, David Dunning and Justin Kruger published a paper that documented how people who don't know much about a given set of cognitive, technical, or social skills tend to grossly overestimate their prowess and performance. Subsequent studies by them and others confirmed this phenomenon.

College students who received poor grades, elderly who unsuccessfully applied for a new drivers' license, investors who declared bankruptcy and scored miserably on tests of financial literacy all rated their performance as superior to the results of the objective assessments they were given. In fact, research shows that individuals with less knowledge about a topic are more likely to be confident about their opinions.

In one study, Dunning and Kruger asked survey respondents if they were familiar with certain technical concepts from physics, biology, politics, and geography. Many claimed to recognize real terms, but they also indicated familiarity with concepts that were fictitious. Over 90% of respondents claimed some knowledge of at least one of the nine fictitious concepts. And perhaps worse, the more well-versed respondents considered themselves in a general topic, the more familiarity they claimed with the meaningless terms associated with it in the survey.

It is easy to make fun of the ridiculous ideas that others subscribe to, but all of us run the risk of falling prey to unrecognized ignorance if we do not apply the C² Factor to ourselves. We need to be curious about the limits of our accumulated experience and knowledge and have the courage to face those limits by responding, "I don't know," when challenged about the things we know for sure.

3. Extending Self-awareness beyond 15 Minutes

One of my favorite exclamations came from a newly appointed executive who hired me to help him acclimate to his new role. I asked him about soliciting feedback from his peers. "I don't need to," he told me, "I know what my blind spots are." The absurdity of his statement apparently escaped him.

In fairness to him, however, he had reason to believe he knew how others perceived him. He had received the so-called 360-degree feedback on that not long before. Looking at it from the outside as we are now, the problem is obvious. Circumstances had changed dramatically for him. He had new peers with likely different standards and his sense of himself had likely also changed at least somewhat. If you asked him, however, my client would have told you that he highly values feedback and invites it often. Moreover, he would not have been lying.

What was going on? My client was demonstrating a phenomenon first identified by Chris Argyris[8] and Donald Schon in 1974 – that there is a discrepancy between what individuals and organizations say governs their behavior and what really governs their behavior. Argyris and Schon called this the "espoused theory" versus the "theory-in-use" in action. Theories-in-use are usually unconscious but nonetheless guide our behavior as opposed to the explanations we give ourselves and others.

It takes courage to look at our behavior and ask ourselves if it matches what we believe about ourselves. When I was president of the board of a small charitable foundation, I was clear about my vision that the group work cooperatively, with respect for each other's opinions and competencies. When I complained that members did not take more responsibility for evaluating the grant proposals we received, it was gently pointed out to me that I often expressed my opinion early and strongly. Believe me, it took courage to be curious about other ways my behavior was getting in the way of how I espoused I wanted the group to work together.

To be champion leaders, we need the C² Factor to repeatedly ask for feedback and truly reflect on how we can use the information about ourselves that we receive.

ENRICHING YOUR LIFE WITH THE C² FACTOR

So far, this chapter has focused on how the C² Factor is useful for self-development – to make us better leaders, partners, friends, and community members. It has focused on staying calm, in touch with our feelings, and aware of the limitations of our thoughts so that we can make astute decisions and take judiciously bold action. And of course, being centered and not dictated to by our thoughts and emotions feels good too. In this section, the emphasis is on how the C² Factor directly enriches our lives.

1. Inspiring Competence

It has already been noted that curiosity is linked to academic achievement. It is also related to the enjoyment of learning. When we are motivated to learn about something because of our curiosity, versus some external reason, we are more engaged, and delight in the process. Neuroscience research has demonstrated that the neurons that fire when we are curious also fire when we anticipate reward. And when we acquire new information, our brains are flooded with dopamine – the pleasure-inducing neurotransmitter. In addition, the part of the brain that is associated with curiosity is also associated with retention of learning.

But competence doesn't develop simply from the acquisition of knowledge. To be competent means to be able to apply that knowledge in a meaningful way. That's where the courage component of the C² Factor comes in. To develop new capabilities, we need to push through the period when we are amateurish or inadequate. We need to risk looking foolish in order to grow.

Think of the elation you felt that last time you were successful using a new skill – public speaking, sailing, hitting that great golf shot, writing an article that was well received – that was the result of the C² Factor in action.

2. Opening to Where You Haven't Been, and What You Haven't Done

The C² Factor gets us out of our cognitive ruts and routinized daily lives where time passes quickly and imperceptibly. In order to bring creativity and mental flexibility to our leadership and our lives, we need to put ourselves in situations where our customary way of responding doesn't apply. Using the C² Factor, we try things we might never have thought of trying before.

So many of the champion leaders I interviewed came from outside the United States and many talked about the value they continue to place on travel to different countries. When we experience a new culture, we have to call on the C² Factor to navigate different requirements and take advantage of new opportunities. When we are amazed by the things we see, we stimulate new parts of the brain that reinvigorates our lives.

The C² Factor inspires us to try new activities. When we do something we've never done before, we naturally have the beginner's eyes we discussed earlier. Novelty can be uncomfortable at first, but because of the synergy inherent in the C² Factor, doing something unusual acts like curiosity fertilizer. "The more you interact with new experiences or information, the more you realize you don't know, which makes further exploration more attractive," says Todd Kashdan,[9] a curiosity expert.

Have you ever noticed how many senior executives are adventuresome in their private lives? Champion leaders seek ways to stay open and curious about different ways of seeing the world that often require a great deal of courage. Richard Branson, founder of the Virgin Group which has a controlling interest in over 400 companies and whose net worth is over $4 billion, is well known for flying hot-air balloons across the Atlantic, skiing down dangerous mountains, and power boat racing. Former CFO of Intel's Internet of Things Group and current CFO of NeoPhotonics, Elizabeth Eby's hobby is underwater photography – frequently of sharks. It is not coincidental that publications designed for senior executives are replete with advertisements for "adventure tourism."

Using the C² Factor to have new experiences shakes us out of our comfort zones, connects us with parts of ourselves that we haven't used recently, and gives us a new perspective on life. These experiences come with significant, tangible benefits to intellectual and physical health, and open our minds to new possibilities for ourselves and our organizations. It is impossible to know if what we discover will be useful in the future but expecting to see something new helps us notice novelty when it shows up.

What have you tried lately? Last year I tried ax throwing. You never know when something useful might show up!

3. The Antidote to Boredom and a Key to Happiness

We can't be swimming with sharks, bungee jumping, and traveling to exotic places all the time, but the C² Factor can help us stay interested in life. We can pay attention to small everyday things and be curious about them instead of reverting to autopilot.

Author of 13 books, a musician, a consultant, and for many years part of senior management of the Meredith Publishing Group, James Autry has many examples of curiosity and courage, including when his wife, Sally Pederson, was lieutenant governor of Iowa.

> I took on the household duties and the care of our autistic son. It was a wonderful period of my life. I went to track meets and teacher conferences and I did the laundry. I got to where I loved taking clothes out of the dryer. I realized how everything can be a rich experience if you open yourself up to what that experience can be.

Jim had the courage to step away from a lucrative career where he was a champion leader to make this change and he brought his curiosity to enrich the experience.

Research shows that simply being curious is associated with a happier and more satisfied life. This is true for adolescents, adults, and older adults. Adolescents with high degrees of curiosity have higher levels of life satisfaction. They have a greater sense of purpose in life and hope than adolescents with both low and average curiosity. There is also evidence that maintaining curiosity in old age is protective against cognitive and physical decline. Compared to the incurious, older adults who score high in curiosity tend to perform better on tests of memory and general cognitive functioning.[10]

We all have the C² Factor, but when we exercise it, we grow those capacities and enrich our lives. YY Lee, the tenaciously curious champion leader we met in Chapter 1, who has served as CEO, COO, public board member, GM, and product leader across a variety of companies, understands the dangers of falling back on the usual ways of doing things. She stimulates her C² Factor and enriches her life by challenging herself to change up such everyday activities as playing with her kids. When COVID restricted their activities, she decided to play ping pong with them using her non-dominant hand. A small change like this challenges the well-worn neuro pathways and builds new ones.

Other ways we can access the C² Factor and reinforce the habit of curiosity and courage are activities such as trying a new hobby, for example:

- Beekeeping (like former Twitter CEO, Dick Costolo)
- Setting a goal and stating it publicly
- Expressing an opinion that is different from our peers
- Being more authentic with others
    or if you're not so adventuresome,
- Learning to play bridge (like Bill Gates)

These small everyday activities build our curiosity and courage, strengthening the muscle of the C² Factor.

In Chapter 1, I warned of the pitfalls of emulating the random curiosity of the 3-year-old mind. However, in this situation – when we're combating boredom and seeking the novel in our daily lives as a path to more joy – it makes a lot of sense. The trick to getting value out of the 3-year-old type of thinking is to focus on that profound curiosity. You may be aware of the "5 Whys" as an approach to problem-solving or strategy development. It is a process of asking a series of "Why" questions. This is a form of that focused profound curiosity.

"Why" also is a litmus test of your own curiosity. If you aren't continuously asking "why?" you are not engaging your curiosity. One senior-level executive client explained to me, "I tell my teams daily, the most important word you use is 'why.' If you're doing something but you can't answer 'why', you shouldn't be doing it." By having the courage to be curious about our habits, we discover the values we are enacting with those routines and perhaps alternative ways to fulfill those values.

And speaking of being on cruise control and getting stuck in routines, we can also use the C² Factor to avoid that fate in our relationships and stay happily married for 50 years – in the next chapter.

NOTES

1. https://peakwellnessco.com/ceos-that-meditate-at-work/.
2. https://news.harvard.edu/gazette/story/2018/04/harvard-researchers-study-how -mindfulness-may-change-the-brain-in-depressed-patients/.
3. Harris, Russ. *ACT Made Simple*. Oakland, CA: New Harbinger Publications, 2009.
4. Bourton, Sam, Lavoie, Johanne, and Vogel, Tiffany. "Leading with Inner Agility." *McKinsey Quarterly*, March 2018. https://www.mckinsey.com/business-functions/ organization/our-insights/leading-with-inner-agility.
5. https://www.nytimes.com/2021/06/30/us/politics/donald-rumsfeld-dead.html.
6. Dunning, David. "We Are All Confident Idiots." *Pacific Standard*, October 14, 2017. https://www3.nd.edu/~ghaeffel/ConfidentIdiots.pdf.
7. Kruger, Justin, and Dunning, David. "Unskilled and Unaware of It: How Difficulties in Recognizing One's Own Incompetence Lead to Inflated Self-Assessments." *Journal of Personality and Social Psychology* 77, no. 6 (1999): 1121–1134. https:// www.gwern.net/docs/psychology/1999-kruger.pdf.
8. Argyris, C., & Schon, D. (1974). Theory in practice: Increasing professional effec- tiveness. San Francisco: Jossey-Bass.
9. Silva, Paul, and Kashdan, Todd. "Interesting Things and Curious People: Exploration and Engagement as Transient States and Enduring Strengths." *Social and Personality Psychology Compass* 3, no. 5 (2009): 785–797. https://doi.org/10.1111 /j.1751-9004.2009.00210.
10. Sakaki, Michiko, Yagi, Ayano, and Murayamaab, Kou. "Curiosity in Old Age: A Possible Key to Achieving Adaptive Aging." *Neuroscience & Biobehavioral Reviews* 88 (May 2018): 106–116.

4

People Who Need People: The Alchemy of Relationships with the C² Factor

Relationships are the foundation of both our personal and professional lives. The better and stronger they are, the more meaning and value they offer. Great relationships are vital for a leader to get things done as well as for personal health and happiness. Curiosity and courage are key building blocks for those healthy relationships. Bringing curiosity to business relationships allows us to explore opportunities for collaboration or see differing perspectives that might not be immediately apparent. That exploration conveys respect and trust, keys to healthy relationships and personal growth. When the going gets tough and there is conflict or discord between partners, team members, stakeholders, or friends, courage is the game changer that enables the curiosity necessary for finding lasting solutions and reaping benefits from these situations.

"My new investor wasted so much time analyzing," the director of the venture capital department of a large utility company complained to me. The director explained:

> But I knew the deal was never going to fly. He focused all his efforts on research and technology and ignored the people – the relationship – part of the equation. I realize he's new, but he did not get buy-in from our internal stakeholders. When I embark on a deal, I don't spend much time doing research myself. I have a network of people I have known since business school who can give me the information I need. And I know from experience that what makes companies succeed or fail is not the technology, it's the management. You are betting on the people.

DOI: 10.4324/9781003212881-4

The new investor had failed to see the value of relationships. He conducted his own research instead of tapping a personal network of experts. He ignored the internal politics that influence the success of any new undertaking, and he had focused on the technology in the target company instead of its management.

Building and maintaining strong, trusted relationships is essential for success. Getting things done requires high levels of coordination and collaboration, which depend on many different types of relationships. In today's flattened and matrixed organizations, this means persuading and influencing others to support your work. Selling ideas, accessing resources, inviting participation are all processes not events. Collaborative relationships are the supply chain of human and social capital needed for creativity.

Relationship management is a large part of emotional intelligence, a hot leadership topic even though it is a concept that has been around for 25 years. Articles abound in the media about the importance of executives demonstrating emotional intelligence and it is often cited as being at least as important as IQ for champion leadership.

As Megan Beck[1] and Barry Libert suggest in their 2017 *Harvard Business Review* article, "The Rise of AI Makes Emotional Intelligence More Important," if professionals want to remain relevant, they need to focus on understanding, motivating, and interacting with human beings. Technology may be able to replace human analysis of complex business problems, for example, but it won't be able to replicate leadership skills such as inspiring engagement, influencing stakeholders, or modeling the values of the desired corporate culture.

A champion leader must be able to effectively build relationships and connections across video screens, emails, texts, and social media posts as well as face-to-face. Additionally, champion leaders must be masters of two types of relationships: one-on-one and groups. These groups may be large, like an all-employees' town hall, or relatively smaller, like a division leadership team or board of directors. But the most important relationships are not with groups, they are between individuals. And for these relationships, the C² Factor is essential.

We are social creatures. The quality of our relationships has a profound impact on our health and happiness. An abundance of research indicates that satisfying relationships not only make people happy, but are also associated with better health and even longer life.[2] Research also shows that curiosity is associated with both happiness and better relationships, so we know that at least one aspect of the C² Factor is at play.

Finally, and eminently, important for leaders is that strong relationships make us better leaders because they keep us on track and make us more effective in achieving results. YY Lee, who as I've mentioned before has an illustrious record of launching and leading enterprise-scale technology businesses with impressive market and P&L results, talked to me about partnering with CEOs and other C-level executives:

> I can be a terrific counterpart to those who are so action oriented that they may fire before they aim, where I can purposely and deliberately take the opposite role. I observe, analyze, calibrate, optimize. It takes courage to willingly take on that role and be the one who says "I'm going to be thoughtful about this" when everyone else is driving to immediate action. In many situations, I am that driver but when I am on a leadership team that is overloaded with energy toward action, I am willing to hold the energy and space to create a balanced tension and a more thoughtful approach. Establishing these types of relationships that consist of balance counterparts and create creative tension are critical to success.

This kind of strong, balancing relationship is what keeps us and companies on track.

In addition to bolstering health and happiness and providing balance for our leadership skills, there are myriad pitfalls that strong relationships can help us avoid. Neuroscientists have identified the "hubris syndrome," a disorder that results from having attained and held power that has been associated with tremendous success for a number of years.[3] Leaders with the hubris syndrome demonstrate exaggerated pride, overwhelming self-confidence, and contempt for others. We may think we are immune but in scientific studies, participants who were artificially placed in powerful positions made less eye contact and tended to interrupt those who were less powerful than them.

If you want to make sure you're not one of those powerful jerks, you need to have strong relationships characterized by both curiosity and courage. When we are fortunate enough to have a committed partner, a loyal friend, or a strong relationship with a business colleague, someone who will tell you when you have spinach on your teeth, we can avoid this disorder and many other pitfalls. Each partner engages an element of the C^2 Factor – one to have the courage to confront and the other the curiosity to listen. For former PepsiCo CEO and Chairman Indra Nooyi, it was her mother who told her to "leave that damn crown in the garage" as she returned from work, having just been appointed Chairman of the Board. For Winston Churchill, it was his wife who chided him when he became excessively hard on people. For several of my clients, it is their children who adore their parents but don't hesitate to tell them about their failings.

Having established the benefits of strong relationships, we can turn to examining how curiosity and courage are essential for their development and maintenance.

WHEN FIRST WE MEET: APPLYING THE C² FACTOR TO BUILD RELATIONSHIPS

1. Empathy without Curiosity Is Merely Projection

The concept of emotional intelligence (EQ) has become an assumed element of leadership. Chapter 2 addressed how the C² Factor aids two components of emotional intelligence – self-awareness and self-management. The other two components of EQ are social awareness and relationship management. The C² Factor is central to these skills as well.

Social awareness is the ability to understand another person's perspective and to empathize with how they are feeling. The ability to empathize is fundamental to all productive relationships. It goes without saying, in personal relationships empathy is the glue that keeps us together.

Empathy, understanding others' perspectives, has also been embraced as an essential leadership skill, as evidenced in the business press. A typical example is the 2016 *Wall Street Journal* article entitled "Companies Try a New Strategy: Empathy Training." Another example is an article for Wharton Business School in which Mark Leiter,[4] former CSO of the Nielson Company, asserts that "empathy is essential for crafting strategy."[5] And Microsoft CEO Satya Nadella[6] claims that empathy has been "the spark for innovation that turned Microsoft around."

Have you ever been told "I know how you feel," and thought "you most certainly do not?" I know I have. To me it feels worse than having the other person ignore my feelings. I remember years ago when I had breast cancer, well-meaning friends would say something like, "I know how you feel. My Aunt Betty had cancer and she …" I did not feel understood. The same thing sometimes happens when coaches who have been senior executives in the past "empathize" with their clients by imagining they are having the same experience that they did. The only way to have true empathy is to have curiosity. So-called "empathy" without curiosity is merely projection.

"Projection" is the psychological term that refers to the universal tendency of people to attribute to others what is in their own minds. That is, we see ourselves in others. This is the basis for empathy, but it can also be the basis of hatred! When we are unaware of our own negative feelings, we can sometimes imagine we see them in others. For example, the cheater who imagines he is always being cheated. Or more benignly, imagining we understand some else's pain because we too have felt pain in what we think is a similar situation. It is not ill intended, merely ill informed.

So how do we know if we are really being empathetic or merely projecting? By using the empathy equation:

$$empathy = projection + curiosity$$

The only way to harvest the empathetic benefits of projection and avoid the possible misunderstanding and distortions of projection is to cultivate curiosity. Remind yourself when you imagine what other people are thinking and feeling, this is a cue to engage your curiosity to ensure you meet the moment with true empathy not merely projection. Surprisingly, perhaps this is often easier to do when relationships are relatively new.

2. Newness + the C^2 Factor = The Honeymoon

Do you remember when you first met your significant other? The intense curiosity you had about them? The delight at being the object of the other's curiosity? The spirit of adventure you felt, the courage to do new things just because you had that new partner. How every experience was enhanced?

When relationships are new, we know that there is a lot we don't know about the other person and as a result, our curiosity can be more easily engaged. We ask them questions – in business we ask about how they view situations in their department, what they envision for the future, perhaps something about their personal life. In our personal lives, we want to know everything about them – where they grew up, what their family was like, what kind of music they prefer, do they enjoy certain foods? Our curiosity invites the person we are getting to know to share information about themselves. If we engage our courage and follow-up by disclosing something about ourselves, the reciprocity contributes to growing the relationship.

Curiosity about other people conveys interest and builds trust. My colleague tells a story about how a woman she had met at a party told everyone else there what a wonderful new acquaintance she had made. My colleague (the wonderful new acquaintance) had spent the entire time asking this woman about herself. Research confirms that this is not just anecdotal. In study after study, Todd Kashdan[7] and his colleagues have shown that curious people are rated more positively in social encounters.

Sometimes, however, it can be difficult to be curious. If someone is too different from us perhaps by status, ethnicity, culture, or seems intimidating in some way, we need the courage of the C² Factor in addition to our curiosity to pursue those relationships. A former client of mine talked about how timid she first was in approaching a new board member. He had come from a high-profile organization and was rumored to be a "superstar."

"I just assumed he was completely comfortable in his new role, but when I finally talked with him, he had so many questions I could help him with. We became fast friends."

Relationships are the foundation of both our personal and professional lives. When we bring curiosity and courage to business relationships, we explore opportunities for collaboration and synergies that might not be immediately apparent. We convey respect and build trust. And we have richer personal lives.

3. Networking without the C² Factor Doesn't Work

One of my business colleagues says she never "networks," but she gets referrals for business, recommendations for resources, information about new opportunities, advice for managing challenges, and new personal connections wherever she goes – the soccer field, the local florist, her hairdresser, the medical practice she uses as well as at business meetings, professional conferences, and community events she attends. Other than speed dating, networking is the one activity in which we are explicitly focused on forming relationships. That may make it sound like a mechanized process, but I would argue that my colleague is networking all the time.

My colleague's high C² Factor leads her to make personal connections and form relationships wherever she goes. She is interested in and curious about everyone she meets and is courageous about engaging them in conversation. She sometimes asks questions that startle me, but her courage seems to charm the people she meets.

In a recent talk at Stanford University, Amy Chang, an executive vice president at Cisco, spoke about the value of networking with curiosity.[8] In her talk, she encourages investing time in people we meet who we find interesting because these relationships will "bear fruit" in unexpected ways.

"I genuinely like people … I am an extrovert, and I am curious about other human beings. If you approach it from a kind of standpoint of genuine curiosity about people, everybody has something to teach you, regardless of who they are, they have something to teach you … whether it's about life, about work or whatever. So, when you sit down with them what you're really trying to figure out is, what does this person have to teach me? And based on my experience, what do I have to help them with?" She maintains that every opportunity she's had to sit on a board has come as a result of one of these serendipitous moments.

And she chose board members for her various companies that way as well – with curiosity and courage. She was curious about how they handled situations, what they thought of certain issues, and what recommendations they might make regarding certain types of opportunities. She also had the courage to interview 26 other CEOs who had worked with these potential board members to understand their experience with the candidates, particularly when they failed.

Whether it's a new business connection or a more personal one, inevitably the excitement wears off and, unfortunately, all too often, so does the C^2 Factor as it applies to the relationship. When the C^2 Factor fades, we lose the richness that it can bring to us – materially, emotionally, and even spiritually.

WHEN THE BLOOM IS OFF THE ROSE: APPLYING THE C^2 FACTOR TO MAINTAIN RELATIONSHIPS

1. They Aren't Cars; They're Gardens

Formerly, the metaphor I used for relationships is that they are like cars. You find a good one, learn how it functions, and except for occasional tune-ups, expect that it will keep operating at a high-performance level. I assumed that once things were "worked out," I could move on to focus on important issues in business and life. However, that was the wrong metaphor.[9] Relationships are much more like gardens, they need tending. Having planted the seeds, we need to make sure they have adequate sunshine and hydration and are fertilized with curiosity.

Once we have gotten to know someone, we tend to lose some of our curiosity about them. We assume we know their relevant strengths and weaknesses, their desires and preferences, their interests and activities. Whether it is a member of the leadership team, your counterpart in another division, or a personal relationship, we often assume, perhaps unconsciously, that they are the same as they were when we first got to know them. We know that over time we grow and change, but somehow we forget that is true of others. We need to continue to be curious about the people in our world or we will be interacting with someone who no longer exists!

I remember working with a leadership team in which two of the members had a falling-out with each other and were having a difficult time working together. In exploring this with them, we discovered that they were each making assumptions about the other based on conversations they'd had when they first met about their political party affiliations. The political atmosphere in the country at the time was exacerbating the situation. Neither had had the curiosity or courage to broach the sensitive topics they assumed were dividing them. Surprisingly, once they'd had a conversation (or several), they discovered that their opinions were not so far apart, and they could respect each other's perspectives.

When I was a couples' therapist, the absence of the C² Factor in a couple's relationship was frequently at the heart of both the boredom that set in and unresolved issues. Partners stopped asking each other about their changing interests, what they thought about the movies they watched, their reactions to current events, etc., because they assumed they already knew. I remember one situation in which the wife had become a vegetarian. The husband assumed it was for health reasons and suggested uber healthy, questionably bland menus on that basis. In reality, the wife had continued to enjoy rich even decadent food. She'd given up meat for humanitarian reasons! Imagine how many uninteresting dinners they'd sat through for no reason!

Blooms inevitably fall off roses, so we need to engage the C^2 Factor to keep the garden producing new blooms. The C^2 Factor provides fertilizer, sunshine, and water, but it also serves another important function that the garden needs – regular weeding.

2. Weeding Your Garden

The nature of a garden is to grow weeds. If no weeds are growing, then conditions are so poor that nothing will be able to grow. However, there is no need to be distressed about problem weeds that crop up in our relationships. Danger only arises when we don't clear them out on a regular basis. Ignored, the weeds can become so large that they choke out the flowers and vegetables. That is why we need to apply our C^2 Factor consistently. Curiosity and courage weed our relationships.

Clearing up misunderstandings, wrong interpretations, unintended oversights require courage and curiosity. I facilitated a meeting of division directors during which one director referred to another director's department as a "black hole." Understandably, that director took offense and initially merely glared at the other. Because he is a champion leader, however, after a few minutes, he had the courage to calmly tell his colleague that it sounded insulting to him and the curiosity to ask him what he meant by the comment. The director who uttered the "insult" was surprised and explained that he had meant only that he didn't understand the processes and objectives of the division.

Imagine the consequences if that leader had not engaged his C^2 Factor and the weed had not been immediately pulled!

3. Tending Someone Else's Garden

Have you been in the position where you see what change needs to be made in your organization, or you know what another leader needs to do to get her team to be more productive, or perceive the best course of action for another person and cannot get acceptance for your ideas? As a coach, an executive, a parent, or a well-meaning friend, it's so frustrating when people don't buy into our ideas or take our advice. Sadly, when faced with this situation, we often try to deal with the situation by explaining our rationale as if they are just not as smart as we are. (Mansplaining is not just for males!)

There are any number of reasons why this occurs (beyond most people's natural inclination to resist being told what to do), all of which can be addressed by engaging our C² Factor.

With the C² Factor, we discover the other person's priorities, concerns, and complications that make taking our advice difficult. Knowing this and having the courage to admit that perhaps we are not so omniscient as we sometimes imagine, we may adjust our recommendations or even admit that they didn't need our advice to begin with.

Good coaches (formal or informal) know that the best way to help another person is to be curious about them and engage their own curiosity about themselves and their situation. What they discover is often far more meaningful than any sage advice that could be given to them. For many of us, courage is necessary for us to keep quiet and resist the urge to prove our worth.

YAY! CONFLICT! USING THE C² FACTOR TO EMBRACE CONFLICT

Not only do other people resist our opinions, at times we find ourselves embroiled in outright conflict with them. Again, not to worry. This is natural in all relationships.

1. We Are All Foreigners

We live in a global economy and much of business is international today, so the idea that different countries have different cultures with unique traditions and norms of behavior is a familiar concept. However, we need to expand this concept to include every person with whom we interact.[10] It is not hard to be curious when we encounter someone from another country, but we need to be equally curious about those we think come from the same background as we do.

Merrill Irving is president and CEO of the largest technical college in Minnesota, Hennepin Technical College, serving over 18,000 students annually. He also is a black, openly gay man, married to a Cuban. Those are just the most surface facts of his life that some might identify as differences and that have contributed to his self-described "courage to question and audacity to push" as he serves diverse learning communities and champions underserved and nontraditional students.

But there is so much more about his background and the development of his thinking to be curious about, including his own remarkable academic career, his acting talent, his time as a competitive tennis player, and how he was raised, to name but a few. Merrill himself has deep curiosity beyond the obvious. As he told me, "When it comes to leadership, I have all the curiosity in the world. I want to know all about you. I want to know where you come from because that goes into trust. I want to know where we are different."

Racial or generational differences are easy to spot, but without the C^2 Factor we will not explore less obvious differences such as life experiences, perceptions, assumptions, and values. We need the courage to address these differences as well. Despite the emphasis on diversity and inclusion today, there remains deep discomfort in addressing racial differences. It is almost taboo to be curious about our dissimilarities.

Generational differences and the assumptions cohorts make about each other manifest in such stereotypes as self-righteous Baby Boomers, skeptical Gen Xers, entitled Millennials, and spoiled Gen Ys. It can be easy to assume that all people born during a certain time frame are universal in their beliefs and behaviors. Without conscious curiosity to investigate and understand the unique qualities of individuals, we run the risk of falling back on these stereotypes to the detriment of our relationships. For example, I know plenty of Boomers who rely on WhatsApp and Millennials who like to talk on the phone.

What is more insidious however is our blindness to the cultural differences between those of us who grew up in the same geographical area, the same region of the country, the same state, the same city, maybe even the same street. We are all from different cultures because we all grew up in different families and have had different life experiences. Recently, a client of mine, the CEO of a mid-size company, mentioned to me that although she'd grown up in the same small town as the COO of the company, she had no idea what the COO's family life was like, their traditions, or their values. Now that is something to be curious about.

What we need to remember is that we usually can't see our own culture. We may see other people's culture, but what we see is "reality or the ways things are." It often doesn't dawn on us that we are looking through the lens of our own culture and may see things differently than others. We interpret their behavior based on assumptions from our own culture and think if we both speak English, we mean the same thing. I worked with two executives who agreed that the organization needed a new people strategy. Much to my surprise, one meant nurturing and developing their current talent, while the other executive meant overhauling management and replacing them with talent from the outside.

Conflict often erupts because of these "cultural" differences, which without our C² Factor can cause us to view the other person as crazy, stupid, or mean. It takes great courage when someone has offended us or vehemently disagrees with us to be curious about their perspective and assume that it has as much validity as ours.

2. Another Damn Growth Opportunity

Conflict in relationships is often an opportunity for growth and development. Human beings tend to be creatures of habit; so if nothing disturbs us, we are likely to remain stuck in our usual ways of doing things. Relationships, however, often disturb us. Partners (of all kinds) complain about how we do things and ask us to change. They have new ideas that challenge ours. Conflict erupts when those challenges confront ideas or methods that are dear to us. It is easy for situations like this to degenerate into a destructive power struggle.

With the C² Factor, however, conflict becomes a growth opportunity. When we are courageous enough to be curious about the challenges our relationships bring, to risk discovering that we were wrong or limited in our thinking, we develop as leaders. We learn to be more inclusive in our thinking and more articulate in communicating it. Change is hard and if we admit it, many of us go kicking and screaming when we are asked to be different in some fundamental way. But if we are lucky enough to have relationships that include the C² Factor, we will be surrounded by people who will be courageous enough to bring to our attention elements of situations we may have missed or ways of being that are less productive than we wish.

3. Neither a Bully nor a Doormat

Most of us may endorse the concept that conflict is good for innovation and creativity, but when it comes to conflict ourselves, we usually have a negative reaction. Our discomfort with conflict is likely due to our early experiences. Growing up, most of us experienced conflict as unsafe. It was either loud and violent or never allowed to emerge. There is no such thing as a conflict-free relationship. If there are two people, there will be differences and therefore conflict. Unfortunately, most of us have few role models for positive conflict.

Our tendencies therefore are to either come out swinging (hopefully metaphorically) or duck and run. Some of us try to pressure the other person into acquiescing by out arguing them, rallying others to our side, or threatening them or warning them of potential danger in not agreeing. Others of us try to avoid conflict at all costs, dodging conversations, pretending the conflict doesn't exist, or saying "yes" to things when we really mean "no." This latter tactic is particularly dangerous. If we comply, we build resentment. Or we resist compliance indirectly and engage in passive aggressive behaviors such as "forgetting," procrastinating, or misplacing important materials.

It takes a powerful C^2 Factor to productively meet intense conflict head-on. There's usually not a bone in our bodies that wants to handle conflict that way, but it is the only way that leads to personal development. I have taken the following process from the Imago couples therapy method to help people benefit from these conflicts. It may seem simple and perhaps not that different from other communication systems, but the small difference makes all the difference. Note the amount of C^2 required.

The person who is most upset about the situation begins by asking the other person to tell him or her how they perceive the situation. Allison and Bob are in a major conflict. Allison is angry and wants to let Bob know how wrong he is. Allison needs to start.

Allison: "Tell me what you see going on and what you think needs to change." As Bob talks, Allison listens and mirrors back what she heard. She tries to use Bob's words and include everything he says.

Allison then asks Bob if she was accurate in what she heard. If Bob says no, Allison asks him to clarify, even if she feels convinced that she got it right the first time.

Allison mirrors again and they go through the same process until Bob says, "yes, you heard me accurately."

Allison then says, "tell me more."

The process continues as above until Bob says, "there's no more."

This can take some extended amount of time and it takes great C^2 Factor on the Allison's part to be open to understanding Bob's perspective, especially if it is dramatically different from her own. Sometimes Bob seems to repeat himself, but it is important that Allison continue mirroring until Bob says there's no more.

I often tell the person in Allison's position that if they want to be heard themselves, there needs to be room inside Bob for him to be able to take in what she is saying. When Bob is so full of his own thoughts, there is no room to take in Allison's.

> Once Bob says that there's no more, he wants to say, Allison summarizes what she's heard.
>
> Allison: "Let me see if I got the most important points that you wanted me to understand …"
>
> If Bob says that Allison understood, they go onto the next step. But if Bob says that Allison missed something important or didn't understand correctly, the process of listening and repeating resumes until Bob is convinced that Allison understands him.
>
> The next step is for Allison to validate Bob's perspective, by saying, "what you've said makes sense to me." She should not say it unless it's true.

Note however, that saying something makes sense does not mean that one agrees, just that the other person is not crazy or malevolent for seeing things the way they do.

> If Allison cannot honestly say that it makes sense to her, she says to Bob, "Help me understand how … ." (the part that doesn't make sense.)

This is not an opportunity to challenge Bob; it is only for Allison's clarification. Whatever new information Bob provides is treated as above.

> After Allison has been able to honestly say "that makes sense to me," she then asks, "would you like to hear how I see the situation?"

It is extremely rare that once a person has been fully listened to, heard, and validated for them to refuse to listen to the other. The roles are then reversed, and Bob does the listening until Allison feels fully heard and validated.

So how does this resolve conflict? Many people ask, "what if the two parties can't agree?" All I can tell you is that in the vast majority of cases, so much new information is revealed, so many more elements taken into consideration, so many solutions emerge that the relationship is solidified or renewed in a way that leads to increased cooperation and expanded collaboration. Champion leaders have sufficient C^2 Factor to be able to execute this powerful process and harness the benefits of conflict.

Champion leaders not only apply the C^2 Factor to their individual relationships, but also know that it is important for creating and maintaining high-performance teams. One example of such an application is in the next chapter.

NOTES

1. Beck, Megan, and Libert, Barry. "The Rise of AI Makes Emotional Intelligence More Important." *Harvard Business Review*, February 17, 2017.
2. Oppong, Thomas. October 18, 2019. "Good Social Relationships Are the Most Consistent Predictor of a Happy Life." Stanford School of Medicine. http://ccare .stanford.edu/press_posts/good-social-relationships-are-the-most-consistent-pre-dictor-of-a-happy-life/.
3. Owen, David and Davidson, Jonathan. "Hubris syndrome: An acquired personality disorder? A study of US Presidents and UK Prime Ministers over the last 100 years." *BRAIN: A Journal of Neurology*, May 2009. https://academic.oup.com/brain/ article/132/5/1396/354862
4. Leiter, Mark. "Crafting Better Strategy: Why Empathy Matters" (former CSO Nielson). March 21, 2019. https://knowledge.wharton.upenn.edu/article/the-empa-thetic-strategist/.
5. Lubin, Joann. "Companies Try a New Strategy: Empathy Training." *The Wall Street Journal*, June 21, 2016.
6. "Microsoft CEO Satya Nadella: How Empathy Sparks Innovation." February 22, 2018. https://knowledge.wharton.upenn.edu/article/microsofts-ceo-on-how-empa-thy-sparks-innovation/.
7. Kashdan, Todd, and Roberts, John E. "Trait and State Curiosity in the Genesis of Intimacy: Differentiation from Related Constructs." *Journal of Social and Clinical Psychology* 23, no. 6 (2004): 792–816. https://doi.org/10.1521/jscp.23.6.792.54800.
8. Chang, Amy. https://ecorner.Stanford.edu/video/networking-with-curiosity.
9. I owe this metaphor to my many mentors and colleagues in the Imago Therapy community, especially Hedy Schleifer from whom I learned so much about intimate relationships.
10. Again, I want to thank Hedy Schleifer whose idea of the country metaphor I am borrowing.

5

High-Performance Teams and Creative Problem-Solving with the C² Factor

The pressure to be constantly brilliant. The risk of bad decisions when making rapid-fire calls. The peril of poor execution when there is limited time to vet ideas and engage others. Typical daily pressures for today's leaders are exhausting and depleting. Champion leaders have found a better way to navigate these treacherous waters. They have the courage to resist solo decision-making, resisting the urge to take action before fully understanding the intricate nature of their challenge, and to engage their curiosity to develop a deeper understanding. They know their real power and greatest potential for successful organizational outcomes lie in their ability to develop and access the wisdom of high-performance teams.

> Joanne, I need your help! If I don't get control of this mountain of classified documents by the end of the month there are going to be serious repercussions. My boss could lose his job. The agency could face criminal penalties! This is a crisis!

Jim,[1] the highly respected SES (Senior Executive Services) Director of a Federal Government agency with an especially sensitive mission, had found the courage to admit he had a problem and, deciding he needed outside help, contacted me. He told me he had developed a solution to his problem, but it would require his team to execute it precisely with no room for error. "I need you to help me get the team aligned," he requested of me.

What was the first thing you did the last time you were presented with a serious problem? If you're like 75% of leaders, you immediately jump into the problem-solving mode, detailing an action list, and delegating

DOI: 10.4324/9781003212881-5

tasks – something Jim was tempted to do in this situation. "And what's wrong with that?" you may ask. After all, we became leaders because of our outstanding problem-solving abilities.

Think about the last time you and others were confronted with a serious issue. Did you calmly evaluate the nature of the threat, or did everyone grab onto a solution, a quick fix, and hang on for dear life?

The challenges you face are complex, there are myriad paths to success, a variety of ways to get to your destination. A seemingly simple example: "how shall we go to Detroit?" Every choice has consequences. Planes can be canceled; trains can run late; driving can be hazardous; walking requires massive energy. Other people have agendas and legitimate self-interests. One has frequent flyer points, another is a railroad buff, a third has a new sports car awaiting a tryout. You can't assume that their interests are the same as your own. No matter how superb your solution is, it is just one option.

Any choice you make runs the risk of being a poor choice if it has come solely from you. Others have not given their perspectives, so your solution may not be adequate for all the elements of the problem, or it may have unintended consequences. Even if your solution is the best course of action, it may not be fully understood by those charged with implementing it, which increases the risk it will be poorly executed, and it may not be truly endorsed by the relevant stakeholders.

By diving in with a solution first, you miss an opportunity to elevate your team's performance and you add to your own exhaustion and stress by pressuring yourself to be constantly brilliant. I had to push Jim to resist the urge to show how smart he was by dictating solutions and help him see he needed to harness the far greater power of his team's collective abilities.

Champion leaders recognize the pitfalls of solo problem-solving. They call upon their C² Factor to develop the most innovative solutions and develop high-performance teams. They use their courage to resist the pressure to take action before they understand the true nature of their challenge. They pause to engage their curiosity to develop a deeper understanding. They have the courage to invite questions about their assumptions and welcome diverse perspectives.

I needed courage to push back on my client Jim, and ask him if he would allow his team to explore a variety of possible solutions. "Are you willing to accept an alternative recommendation if your team comes up with something feasible but different?" I was asking him to be both curious and courageous.

Champion leaders insist that their teams have the courage to own the issues and take responsibility for results. And they encourage them to engage in curiosity before trying to find solutions. These leaders understand that curiosity and courage enhance problem-solving and help develop high-performance teams. They also have the courage to commit to the action necessary to execute on those solutions. To his credit, my client agreed.

It takes courage to be curious about our assumptions, biases, and the limitations of our perspective. Without curiosity, however, our solutions are likely to be uninspired and our teams merely groups assigned to tasks. It takes curiosity-informed courage to take the action necessary to design and implement innovative solutions.

So how do we go about engaging the C^2 Factor with our teams?

SIMPLE BUT NOT EASY

1. Engaging the C^2 Factor

Jim, the director in our example, showed the courage to have curiosity about possible alternative solutions to this crisis and to challenge the team to discover them. I agreed to coach the team to help them reach their goals.

The agency's problem was long-standing and involved millions of dollars of contracts. There had been numerous failed attempts to solve the problem. The failures had been hidden and then ignored over several years. The agency had been subject to public scrutiny for problems in the past and, given the sensitive nature of their work, another exposure of inadequacy was sure to be scandalous.

Additional courage was clearly called for: I needed courage to help the team find a more effective solution and the team members would need courage to face this embarrassing and threatening situation by taking responsibility for the problem and its solution. I came to the first meeting not knowing what to expect.

When I met the team, I was surprised to find that each member of the ten-person team of leaders from across the country had his own lawyer next to him at the table! Seated in leather chairs around a mahogany conference table with yellow legal pads in front of each person, no one made eye contact or greeted each other. The small amount of geniality and normal politeness that was present left the room as Jim closed the door. The only sound was from one young man tapping his pen. The woman I sat next to was bouncing her leg up and down rhythmically. Was she marking the time until she could attack? Anxiety was running high, and trust was low. These people were not a team, but a collection of individuals prepared for combat.

To alter the dynamic of this group and ensure any chance of developing a successful solution, curiosity, in addition to courage, was clearly called for. Why had this challenge become such a huge problem? Why had previous attempts to solve it failed? Why was this group not functioning as a team?

Jim had learned about the extent of this problem shortly after he was appointed to his position – when the auditors arrived. They were followed by warnings of criminal investigation. Jim was reasonably certain that there was no intentional crime, but he did not underestimate the seriousness of the situation. Jim was determined that the approach of hide and ignore would not continue under his watch.

It was clear by the nearly 100 emails that had been exchanged, each cc'd to over 25 people, the presence of the lawyers, and the urgency in the director's voice as he addressed the group, that there was a lot riding on finding a meaningful resolution to this problem.

Once again, Jim's courage enabled us to proceed. With the power of the Senior Executive Service status behind him, he announced, "This meeting is for team members only. Everyone else must leave now." The lawyers were escorted out of the room. He had clearly signaled that this was to be a problem-solving endeavor, not simply a charade to distribute blame, launch recriminations, and provide cover.

Over the first hurdle, Jim needed the team to be curious enough to develop a solution that had thus far eluded this team.

2. Wait … What's the Problem?

It is not profound to say that it's important to diagnose the problem before embarking on finding a solution. Nonetheless, more frequently than we like to admit, we are busy working on solutions before we really know what we are trying to solve. Especially under stress, we like clarity and simplicity. It is easy to resort to simplistic answers and prescriptive strategies when pressed for immediate answers.

Jim and I had decided to use the Action Learning method[2] of problem-solving because it has been shown to be effective in solving complex problems across a wide variety of organizations. It is a somewhat unusual approach in that it emphasizes questions over answers. The method stipulates that statements can only be made in response to a question. I knew that this would call on the C^2 Factor in both the leader and his team. Action Learning prevents grandstanding and debating and engages the members' curiosity. And it requires courage to participate in the process.

As prescribed by the method, the session began with Jim taking five minutes to reiterate the problem and describe the process we would use. As expected, the participants didn't eagerly embrace the process. When faced with a problem to solve, we usually want to "make our case" and be able to explain our views, so it is understandable that most people resist the idea of focusing on the questions. Some may even resent it, but we need to persist if we want to change the dynamics of our teams.

Twenty minutes into the session, I asked each member of the team to write down their understanding of the problem. When everyone had finished, I asked them to go around the room and read only what they had written. Surprise! No one seemed to agree on the nature of the problem. No wonder they previously hadn't been able to find a solution that had staying power. Each person saw the causes and implications quite differently. The questions needed to continue.

3. Beautiful Questions

The session proceeded as team members asked questions to the director and eventually to each other. In Action Learning, anyone can ask a question, and anyone can answer, but debating isn't possible because unless it is a response to a question, members cannot keep asserting their thoughts. By insisting on questions, curiosity in members of the team is stimulated. Instead of spending energy explaining why their solution is correct, they must inquire about the nature of the problem and learn how others see it.

Do you think that is easy? It most certainly is not! It is such an unusual way of interacting around problem-solving that team members initially try strategies to get around the "rule." Like many other groups I have facilitated, the government team began by asking questions like lawyers – and we know that lawyers never ask a question that they don't already know the answer to!

- "Wouldn't you agree that ... ?"
- "Didn't you try that process in your department?"
- "Am I right in saying you are new to this division?"

Another work around technique they used was to make statements that were disguised as questions.

- "Have you thought about trying ... ?"
- "It's important that we stick to established procedures, don't you agree?"

It is not unusual for team members to initially think that limiting their interactions to asking questions or responding to someone else's questions as gimmicky and merely agree to "play along." But as often happens in groups I coach, their inherently competitive spirits got engaged as they interacted with their peers. Members began to want to be the one to ask meaningful questions. They asked:

- What would success look like?
- What do you want to happen?
- What have we tried before? What happened?
- Why have other approaches not been tried?
- What is maintaining the status quo?

Gradually, the team of guarded combatants began asking more thoughtful and improved questions. Team members leaned forward, looked at each other when they talked, and smiled! New information emerged and inevitably as their curiosity was piqued, the team shifted into a genuinely inquiring mode. The leg tapping had stopped; the clock watcher was taking notes; and the team began monitoring themselves on the quality of their questions:

- How have others in our organization viewed this problem?
- What factors contributed to causing this problem?
- What assumptions are we making about our organization?
- What is different now than when this situation began?

The group had begun functioning as a C² Factor informed team. What elements are essential to maintain it?

4. Attitude Is Everything

Early in the session, I had noticed that some people were participating more than others. One woman sat with her head down doodling on her paper. Periodically she would look up, let out a long sigh, and then go back to doodling. An older man sat with his arms crossed, frequently glancing at the clock. I was concerned about their lack of participation and apparent boredom with the process. I was curious. What did this mean? Why were some participating more than others? Was this due to ennui, fear, lack of understanding? Was it the process or were the people somehow flawed?

In my role as coach, however, I also had to limit my interventions to questions. So, I asked the team what they noticed about member participation. They acknowledged that some people had been quiet but minimized its meaning. They all agreed that members would speak "if they had something to say."

How could they not be curious? Was fear getting in the way? What did they know that I didn't? It took courage on my part not to jump in and make it easy to get everyone to participate, to try to "help" the process to success. I had to force myself to resist my own preconceived analysis and engage my curiosity to wonder about what was going on. In order for the group to develop into a true team, and agree on the real problem, it needed to be responsible for its internal processes.

It requires courage to listen to questions, especially when it seems like all questions are challenges to your ideas. And depending on tone and intent, the question "what makes you say that?" can be asked as follows:

- What makes you say *that*? (Such an idiotic idea!)
- What makes *you* say that? (Someone in your position? You idiot.)
- What makes you say that? (I would really like to understand.)

If the motive for a question is only to challenge for the sake of challenging, it will not be any more helpful than an assertion. In these situations, to make the process productive, I coach my clients to not listen too closely to the tone. I tell them to assume benign intent, even or perhaps especially when that might be wrong! Responding to the content helps keep the conversation based in curiosity. That takes courage.

Once energized by curiosity, however, the team at the government agency seemed to enjoy exploring, elaborating on ideas, and seeing what avenues of inquiry the idea opened up. The team interactions were lively. They seemed to feel pleased to be discovering even more possibilities. The foot tapper had taken off her shoes and talked easily with the team member she had glared at earlier. The clock watcher had not even noticed that our time for that day was nearly up! As people seek and find answers, they become energized, absorbed, determined. Doodles and clocks were no longer of interest – their only interest was discovery.

Seven hours after the lawyers had been asked to leave, the team finally agreed on the essential nature of the problem. By being courageous enough to encounter each other and use an unusual process that emphasized quality questions over rapid answers, their curiosity was ignited.

The team was able to understand the complexity of the problem and the unintended consequences of previous attempts at solutions. Their attitude transformed from defensiveness to curiosity and the stalemate was thawed. The group was transforming into a high-functioning team.

As the group at the government agency grappled with the problem facing them using their C² Factor capacity, they were transforming from a group into a true team. Using their curiosity, instead of their judgments about the other members of the group, they got to know each other. They expanded their understanding of the complexity each member had to deal with and because they were not debating, became more collaborative.

"Do you know why I didn't say much at the beginning?," one of the members asked a colleague on the second day. "It was because I was very offended by your characterization of my department as a 'mysterious place.'"

"I only meant that I didn't understand what happened to the information in the documents once it went to your people," he replied. "I am much clearer about our mandates now."

The group used courage to constructively confront each other. I was glad that I had exercised my courage earlier and resisted intervening when I noticed she wasn't participating. They were becoming more than a group of people; they were becoming a high-performance team.

To keep functioning at this high level and to produce an innovative solution, they needed to continually engage the C² Factor. Like most teams I work with, as the process continued, they confronted the issues related to what and who they felt threatened by. They had to consciously commit to practicing curiosity and courage.

WHAT ARE WE AFRAID OF?

1. Silence Is Golden if We Can Tolerate It

Having agreed on the problem, the team then needed to determine what decisions had to be made. Could they agree on what a solution would look like? Having spent the bulk of the first day asking questions to get clarity on the problem, asking questions about a solution seemed relatively easy. However, I was concerned that they had prematurely left curiosity and were moving into certainty. I asked the team to reflect on whether they were ready to move to solution or if there was more to understand.

They responded with stony silence. It had taken courage for me to slow them down in the face of the pressure to produce results, but it took even more courage for us all to resist the urge to immediately fill that uncomfortable space that silence creates. In a 2009 study across five continents and ten languages, Tanya Stivers[3] and her associates found that during usual conversation, the amount of time between one person speaking and another is a minuscule 200 milliseconds. Stretching that gap means breaking norms and creating social discomfort. Believe me, I was feeling that social discomfort!

But it is in that space that new ideas germinate and appear.

Psychotherapists and group process facilitators have long known that silent gaps are exceedingly useful in encouraging reflection, personal responsibility, and flow of ideas. Trainees are encouraged to welcome them. Neuroscientists have identified silence as an essential element of creativity.[4] Silence gaps are the echo chambers of reflection, the recesses of the shrine where deep thinking can occur.

Recently, the business world has begun to recognize the value in silence as well. In their *Harvard Business Review* (2019) article, "The Case for More Silence in Meetings," Steven Rogelberg and Liana Kreamer[5] describe current research that supports the benefits of silence as "one way of better leveraging the ideas, perspectives, and insights of organizational talent." They cite studies that demonstrate that silence allows for unique knowledge and novel ideas to emerge, and that silent brainstorming results in a higher number and better quality ideas.

When I work with leadership teams in multi-day events, I always begin the morning after a working session by asking team members to articulate the problem and the mission of the day as they see it. It no longer surprises me that they come in with different ideas than they'd had the night before. The respite from immediate conversation and the "silence" of sleep have allowed their subconscious minds to percolate. I needed to keep all this in the forefront of my mind as I endured the team's silence.

Finally, one of the team members who had been very quiet for most of the meeting asked, "What if we need two types of solutions – one for our 'hair-on-fire' situation and the other for longer term?" The room erupted in spontaneous conversation. Rapid exchanges about how each of their departments had struggled to get their arms around both aspects of the situation simultaneously flew across the room.

The silence had created room for reflection and the space for a more reticent member of the team to provide a much-needed contribution. Her courage to clarify what they were grappling with sparked more of the team's curiosity. Having the courage to tolerate silence had enriched the problem-solving process.

2. Stupid Questions

It may not seem like it would take a lot of courage to ask questions if they are not challenging the prevailing model or solution, but what about stupid questions? A common aphorism is "there's no such thing as a stupid question," but in real life people can feel pretty stupid asking about something when it appears that it is common knowledge to everyone else in the room. Especially among peers, it is natural to want to appear knowledgeable and competent. To ask a question that exposes a lack of understanding can make one appear weak.

No member of a team wants to look incompetent. In fact, the preeminent executive coach, Marshall Goldsmith[6] reports that the vast majority of over 50,000 leaders he has worked with rate themselves in the top 20% of their peer group. They believe themselves to be extraordinarily competent. Why would they risk appearing to be among the bottom 80%? Popular business books can talk all they want about vulnerability; senior executives get to where they are in part by exuding expertise. It isn't easy to ask that stupid question.

But asking "stupid" questions is invaluable to team problem-solving, so teams need someone courageous enough to do so. One way to combat the fear of stupid questions is to have team members come from diverse parts of the organization. The idea is that someone who is not supposed to be an expert in a particular subject would be more willing to ask a question regarding that subject than another expert would. For example, the VP of marketing could ask a question about supply chain that the VP of procurement would either not think of or be too embarrassed to ask.

The members of the government agency team came from different geographical areas and had different functional responsibilities. As the group began to explore possible solutions, one member asked how a certain process worked. Although there was some eye-rolling before the response, the explanation revealed that more than one team member was unclear about the process. "Wait, that's not why we do it." "Well, if that's why, … what about?" A whole new line of inquiry into possible solutions opened up.

Teams need to be curious and courageous when confronted with silence, inconsistencies, exceptions, and "stupid" questions because they bring high value to the process. They need the C^2 Factor to embrace what they may be afraid of.

In addition to these challenging but enriching occurrences, there are often people on the team who may seem threatening or difficult but are highly valuable. Not surprisingly, they are often not well liked. Most of the team may even want to eject them. The champion leader understands that these members bring special value and ensure their ongoing inclusion.

WHO ARE WE AFRAID OF?

1. Scapegoats

What do Catherine O'Leary, Yoko Ono, Gaëtan Dugas, and William Comey have in common? What about immigrants, Wuhan City, China, and Simba in the movie Lion King? How about that annoying person on your team who always seems to have a contrary opinion? What do they all have in common with each other?

They are all scapegoats. Scapegoats are blamed for negative outcomes that are actually due to complex factors and the actions of a larger group. The group criticizes the scapegoat, thereby explaining their failures without having to explore their own responsibility. If the problem of unemployment is blamed on immigrants or Wuhan is blamed for the pandemic spread, an examination of the larger systemic issues can be avoided.

The scapegoat says things that others in the team are thinking but are afraid to say out loud. Yoko Ono spoke about the Beatles infighting over the distribution of artistic credit and compensation. William Comey announced an investigation into Hillary Clinton's emails, but this issue had been festering for months. Although frequently disliked, the scapegoat serves an important function.

The Federal Government team I described earlier had hired a consultant prior to my engagement who was participating in the problem-solving session. Perhaps because he had not been able to find an adequate solution in the past, he kept reminding them about the complexity of the problem and the cumbersomeness of the federal government system. In addition, he was not "one of them," so was a good candidate to be a scapegoat. Group members started sighing and looking away when he spoke. They glanced at each other and passed notes. They were clearly annoyed. I confess I was glad it was him and not me being scapegoated.

It is understandable that the group would want to do away with a nay-sayer, the wet blanket, the guy who says "but … " Much is written about the dangers of members like this – their impact on team morale, their impediment to progress, their fear of change.[7] We write them off as "resistant" and prefer not to deal with them. We scapegoat them.

When we engage the C² Factor, however, we see their valuable role on the team. With the courage to be curious, we can explore the importance of the issues they raise. We can ask them:

- What factors are we not considering?
- What unintended consequences do you anticipate?
- How might this solution be driven off course?
- What alternatives do you see?

Sometimes the scapegoat is the bravest member of the group. They dare to say, "the emperor has no clothes." Other times the group "assigns" the role to someone. People don't necessarily volunteer. They are singled out because they are different from other members in some particular way. These scapegoats have to reach deep inside themselves to find their courage. Champion leaders recognize this and take action to see that the person remains psychologically safe and respected.

The director of the federal agency supported the consultant's inclusion in the group. He knew that the consultant had a perspective that other members didn't share and that the information he could provide would be useful in designing a robust solution.

2. Eccentrics and Other Difficult People

Leaders with the C^2 Factor listen to people with crazy ideas. In the 1973 movie, *Sleeper*, directed by Woody Allen, a health food store owner who was cryogenically frozen in 1973, is defrosted 200 years later. One of the jokes in the movie involves foods that had become health foods in the year 2173. Foods that we all knew in 1973 were simply indulgences with no nutritional value. Those foods? Wine and chocolate. "Preposterous!" We all laughed. Today dark chocolate and red wine are cited as foods that contribute to longevity.

Richard Stallman[7] is a difficult person. He is opposed to human procreation, makes jokes about rape and abortion, and is known to wear a pin that reads "Impeach God." But in the early 1990s, he was the first person to tout the benefits of open-source technology. When commercial interests became involved in computing, they were primarily concerned with protecting products by hiding their source code and copyrighting their software. Commercial software manufacturers thought it was ridiculous to share their intellectual property and that Stallman's idea was absurd.

Fast-forward to today and open-source technology is common, used by companies such as Google, Mozilla's Firefox web browser, and Apache HTTP web server. While still eschewed by many commercial enterprises, Facebook, Google, and LinkedIn all release their OSS, so developers can share knowledge, innovate solutions, and contribute to stable, functional products.

There weren't any eccentrics on the Federal Government team, and we might have been worse off for it. I don't know. What I do know is that some of the members of leadership teams I have worked with, who I initially found to be the most irritating, have often made important contributions. In this case, it was the woman I approached at the end of our first day of work when I was feeling enthusiastic about what we'd accomplished.

"What do you think?" I asked eagerly.

"Honey," she replied grimly, "I've worked for the Federal government for 25 years with top appointees and I'll believe results when I see them." Though her words stung, they helped me understand how immutable the complex government system can be and how demoralizing that is for leaders trying to innovate. I needed to keep this in mind as I invited them to be innovative.

Leaders who exercise the C² Factor listen to crazy ideas like wine being a health food and to difficult messages. They welcome characters like Richard and other difficult people to their team.

To remain a high-performing team, members need to consciously use their C² Factor. This means moving beyond reacting and adapting to changing conditions. As Wayne Gretzky has said, it means "skating where the puck is going to be," looking for opportunities to innovate. They need to practice the art of using courage and curiosity synergistically.

EXERCISING THE C² MUSCLE

1. Break the Adage

The adage "if it ain't broke, don't fix it" puts our curiosity to sleep and anesthetizes our courage. How many of our current governance and organizational processes that were put in place for very sensible reasons, to meet requirements at the time, have become archaic and hindrances under current conditions?

The Federal Government team discovered that they had all privately questioned some of the arcane procedural requirements of their departments. They had all quietly adapted by creating ad hoc practices to get around the system. This resulted in convoluted processes that led to enormous cost overruns, dubious contracting, and questionable legal tactics. The team needed to question how their usual way of doing business had inadvertently led them into this logistical and legal morass. They needed to be curious about how they had inadvertently created a dysfunctional system. They needed courage to ask these questions of themselves.

By applying their curiosity, the team also came up with sophisticated solutions to the problem they were facing. With courage, they invited the director of the agency back into the meeting to present their recommendations. It was quite different than what he had envisioned.

"Will you be able to fully execute the short-term tactic before the end of the month?"

"We have no doubt we will have it completed by the end of next week. Our long-term strategy will take more time to completely flesh out, but we have committed to meet on a regular basis to finish the process and keep it on track."

The government group had become a high-functioning team, having developed positive collaborative relationships, and taking mutual responsibility for designing and executing innovative solutions. To remain so would require a consistent exercising and thereby strengthening of the C^2 muscle.

2. Practice, Practice, Practice

Research on brain plasticity demonstrates that neuropsychological operations such as the C^2 Factor are like muscles. They grow stronger with use. Moreover, with repeated use, they eventually can become our default way of thinking and behaving. The brain actually grows new neuronal connections through practice. The description neuroscientists use for this phenomenon is "what fires together wires together." To form the C^2 factor, we need courage and curiosity to become wired together.

Once a neural pathway is established, certain situations such as being presented with a complex problem act as cues that trigger a set of responses – asking questions, seeking the perspectives of others, pausing to reflect, looking for the root cause, etc. The success achieved by using this approach is rewarding and as a result the next time the cue is presented, we are even more likely to repeat the process. With practice, neural networks grow new connections and strengthen existing ones. Utilizing the C^2 Factor becomes a habit.

One way to practice is by asking, "what if the opposite were true?" In the Federal Government, it had always been assumed that the best way to contract was by competitive bid. It was further assumed that due to economies of scale, large companies would be more efficient at delivering those goods and services. In several aspects of this complex situation, the opposite turned out to be true. Courage came into play when they had to slay a number of these sacred cows by challenging various procurement leaders.

Consider challenging the following assumptions by asking "what if the opposite is true?"

- Licensing professionals is essential to ensure high-quality services.
- Performance feedback helps improve performance.
- Companies in the same competitive market must compete.
- The primary function of schools is to educate.

Another way teams can practice the C^2 Factor is by asking themselves questions about their assumptions about how they fit into the larger organizational environment and challenge the status quo by asking "what should we be doing differently?" All of the questions that the government team asked as a way of problem-solving can be used on a regular basis to discover opportunities to innovate. The point is not a specific set of questions so much as making the C^2 Factor an explicit value so that it becomes part of the culture.

A significant aspect of courage is the mere willingness to engage one's curiosity, to question the cultural beliefs we take for granted, and to push back on the normative pressures that make us so comfortable belonging to the group. The C^2 Factor is integral to developing and sustaining high-performance teams and for ensuring creative problem-solving. The concept is easy to understand and lip service is often given to its importance, but in the day-to-day routine of leading an organization, it can be hard to manifest.

Champion leaders consciously create conditions in which questions are invited and challengers are welcome. They hold open the space for questions and discussion resisting the urge to act before the true nature of their mandate is understood, modeling this for their teams. The focus of their curiosity and that of the team's, however, is on charting a course of action.

Having seen how important the C^2 Factor is for oneself, one's relationships, and one's team, next we will focus on what the C^2 Factor brings to leading organizations.

NOTES

1. Name changed.
2. Marquardt, Michael. *Optimizing the Power of Action Learning.* Mountain View, CA: Davies-Black Publishing, 2004.
3. Stivers, Tanya, Enfield., Brown, Penelope, Englert, Christina, Hayashi, Makoto, Heinemann, , Trine Hoymann, , Gertie , Rossano, Federico , de Ruiter, Jan Peter, Yoon, Kyung-Eun, and. Levinson,, Stephen C., "Universals and cultural variation in turn-taking in conversation." PNAS, June 30, 2009. www.pnas.org/cgi/doi/10.1073/pnas.0903616106

4. Kounios, John, and Beeman, Mark. *The Eureka Factor: Creative Insights and the Brain.* New York: Random House, 2015. ISBN-10: 1400068541

5. Rogelberg, Steven G., and Kreamer, Liana. "The Case for More Silence in Meetings." *Harvard Business Review,* June 14, 2019. https://hbr.org/2019/06/the-case-for-more -silence-in-meetings.

6. Goldsmith, Marshall. *What Got You Here Won't Get You There.* New York: Hyperion, 2007.

7. https://en.wikipedia.org/wiki/Richard_Stallman.

6

Champion Leadership with the C² Factor

The alchemy is where the magic is. Curiosity and courage are staple traits among desired attributes in a leader, but champion leaders embrace the powerful effect of the alchemy of the two. They understand that deliberately calling upon these traits, one flowing to the other and back in a continuous loop, is essential for any leader who wants his organization to nimbly navigate the lightning-speed change of today and be prepared for an assuredly uncertain future. Where are you in the quadrants of curiosity and courage? What leadership traits do you have, molded by organizational life, that get in the way of exercising curiosity and courage? How can the C² Factor impact strategic thinking, current models of leadership, and even the agile leader?

While both curiosity and courage are staple traits found on any list of desired leadership qualities, it is the alchemy of the two that champion leaders embrace. The C² Factor is not the only characteristic of champion leadership, but it is essential for any leader who wants his organization to nimbly navigate the lightning-speed change of today and be prepared for an assuredly uncertain future. That is the world in which we operate. The C² Factor is often interwoven with many vital qualities of excellent leaders – integrity, accountability, resilience, strength, and resourcefulness, to name but a few. It may even be seen as a gateway to other leadership competencies, providing the motivation for learning and the impetus for action.

DOI: 10.4324/9781003212881-6

WHO DO YOU WANT TO BE?

1. The C² Leader Diagnostic

What type of leader are you going to be? It's your decision to make. Look at Figure 6.1 and ask yourself which of the four types of leaders you want to become:

Robotic leaders keep their heads down, focus on what they've always done best. They use the same technology, the same organizational structure, and the same view of their customers they've had for five years. Remember Jeff Immelt, the former CEO of GE who refused to listen to those around him and insisted on continuing business as usual despite deep problems at the company?

Reckless leaders take action but fail to use curiosity to understand alternative options, the opinions of others, or the complexities of the situation like Travis Kalanick, former CEO of Uber, who lumbered through situations forcing his desires on others, often women and even European cities.

Academic leaders love exploring ideas and engaging their curiosity, but fail to engage the courage necessary to make tough decisions and to

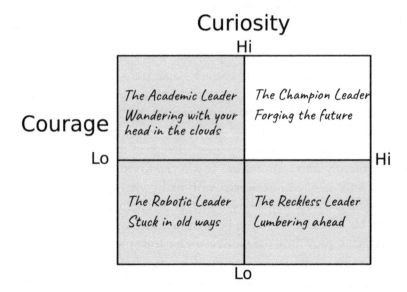

FIGURE 6.1
C² quadrant.

take action, like President Jimmy Carter who was seen by many as more interested in creating the best procedures and methods for making policy than in actually implementing it.

2. Champion Leaders

Champion leaders embrace the C^2 Factor, the alchemy of curiosity and courage. Curiosity helps ensure an appreciation for the complexity of decisions, and courage enables one to decide in the face of ambiguity. Champion leaders know that all the great ideas in the world are merely flights of fancy if they are not put into action. They want to see curiosity manifested in the marketplace and they understand courage is required to get there.

Richard Branson[1] is such a champion. Branson showed courage early in life by overcoming dyslexia and poor academic achievement to become one of the most successful businessmen of our time. His curiosity is evident in the broad range of industries his companies represent. Beginning with Virgin Records, he went on to found Virgin Airways, Virgin Railgroup, Virgin Galactic, and many others. He's had telecom ventures, media investments, and interests in hotels, healthcare, and charitable undertakings.

It is easy to see his courage in the kind of hobbies he enjoys – hot air ballooning, ocean sailing, kitesurfing, and, currently, space travel! But his courage underlies his business dealings as well. For example, his early success with Virgin Records was due in part to his willingness to sign controversial musical groups such as the Sex Pistols and unknowns such as Culture Club.

Champion leaders also know that curiosity is to courage as mindfulness is to agility. Curiosity and mindfulness can be thought of as descriptions of inner states, while courage and agility are ways of behaving.

"I live curiosity and courage every day. They're essential to what I do. In fact, if those qualities weren't part of my DNA, I'm not sure I'd be where I am today," Jacqueline Guichelaar, Group CIO for CISCO told me:

> I'm always curious to understand what I don't know and if there's a better way to do things. I'm the person in the room asking the hard questions, the ones no one else wants to ask or might be afraid to hear the answers to. The power of curiosity is not in finding the perfect answer. It's the willingness to look at things differently, to challenge your assumptions, and to ask why – not just of others, but also of yourself.

Jacqueline has equal part courage as well. While an executive at IBM in Australia, she was offered a position at Deutsche Bank to lead a transformation the company had never done before. She would be the leader of an organization of 2,000 German men (and a few women). "I had to ask myself if I had the courage to take that job, in a country where I knew no one, wondering if I would be ready." Apparently, she was ready. She went on to CIO roles at Deutsche Bank, Lloyds Banking Group, and Thomas Reuters before coming to CISCO.

The C^2 Factor creates a tolerance for ambiguity and a willingness to explore seemingly unrelated ideas to form new synergies of innovation. From that state of mind, a leader has the courage to act without the full knowledge of all the variables, but with a sense of what's right regardless of the personal cost. They are agile, without being unduly influenced by either outside threats or momentary rewards. And they respond to the business and personal environment with equanimity.

It's not surprising that most of us want to be champion leaders who embrace that alchemy of curiosity and courage. Without the C^2 Factor, we run the risk of being leaders who are robotic, academic, or reckless. With the C^2 Factor, we can be champions.

BUSINESS AS USUAL GETS IN THE WAY

If the C^2 Factor makes leaders superior and most of us admittedly want to be champion leaders, why isn't everyone using it? The short answer is, the concept may be simple, but it's not easy. As leaders become more senior, organizational demands encourage behavior that gets in the way of accessing the C^2 Factor. Champion leaders recognize this and take steps to mitigate the impact of those demands.

1. Too Busy

Remember the executive in Chapter 3 who had done a day's work before 8:30 a.m. and would answer the day's accumulated emails until midnight? She is one of many executives I have worked with to reduce the volume of activities clamoring for their attention and focus on those representing the most meaningful contribution to their organizations.

These executives had the talent and the capacity to be champion leaders but were simply too busy to call upon their C^2 Factor to assess which activities were essential and which were needlessly eating their time. Time that could be better spent focused on larger issues of leadership such as strategic decision-making.

Ending the meeting madness and lassoing unruly email: addressing mundane, day-to-day activities may seem trivial, but simple tactical changes in managing these time-consuming activities can have profound effects. Research has shown that what distinguishes high-performing leaders from average leaders has more to do with their daily routines than any set of so-called leadership competencies.

Often, I make tactical suggestions intended to help create the space necessary to be curious and make courageous decisions. One of the first is usually to assess which of those back-to-back meetings a leader really needs to attend and which may be declined. When asked to think about it, leaders easily recognize which are which. Compounding the loss of time to meetings, executives also lose hours preparing materials – often in the form of the dreaded power point deck. I was astounded to learn that one senior VP had produced a 15-slide deck filled with facts, figures, and time-consuming analyses for a 30-minute meeting!

I have also coached very capable leaders, who have no time to catch their breath, on how to manage emails. It is not surprising, given a leader may easily receive 300 emails a day. One simple but often overlooked tactic is to ask those who send emails to indicate in the subject line whether the intent is to

- inform,
- request input or feedback,
- request resources, or
- ask for approval.

This method helps the recipient, but it also helps the author of the email as they reflect on exactly why they are sending it. I have often been surprised when the sender themselves are not clear in their own mind. As a leader, you can cascade this practice throughout the organization, benefiting everyone and creating more space for individuals to step back and be curious about the world beyond their immediate environment and how it might inform their work and their lives.

Relinquish the details: Every leader understands that delegating is essential to being effective, but as a matter of practice, it is easier said than done. Champion leaders have learned that their C^2 Factor can help them more effectively delegate. Engaging their curiosity allows them to see their direct reports in a new light, understand their capabilities more completely, and subsequently explore new options for structuring work. And, by engaging their courage, they are able to let go of the perceived need to touch every initiative in their department.

One of my favorite clients, Larry, is the COO of a large nonprofit organization. He is deeply committed to the organization and its humanitarian mission, but he was profoundly exhausted. The organization was going through a substantial change initiative, and he was an integral part of the process – too integral. I asked him when he had time to think, and he sheepishly acknowledged that it was only on his drive home, usually after 9:00 p.m. When he was a lower level manager, Larry had vowed that he would not be "one of those leaders" who demanded performance from his direct reports without doing hard work himself. He saw "rolling up his sleeves" as a way of supporting his people.

I helped him see that he was inadvertently creating dependency and getting in the way of his reports' growth opportunities. Seeing it from that perspective, he readily began relinquishing his need to be so involved. Larry became a champion leader engaging his C^2 Factor to be curious about his motivation and the impact of his behavior and then had the courage to challenge his assumptions and change his leadership style. Larry began carving out time for reflecting, thinking strategically, and making decisions. He became the champion leader he was meant to be.

2. Too Expert

It is a common practice for companies to groom their "high potentials" – those they anticipate promoting to more senior leadership positions – by exposing them to different facets of the business. These "hi-po's" frequently do rotations of 18 months or so in different divisions of the enterprise in order to be a leader who is "well-rounded." Despite these experiences, however, a leaders' original discipline often has a lasting influence on their perspective. An engineer almost always thinks first like an engineer; a marketing leader will usually think first about marketing; those with a finance background approach situations with the balance sheet in mind.

Leaders can easily fall into the trap of relying on their expertise. After all, their superior performance no doubt accounts for their promotion.

Champion leaders recognize this tendency and combat it in two primary ways: (1) with zig-zag career paths and (2) by seeking and welcoming information – even challenging or difficult information.

Zig zag careers: It was striking to me how many of the champion leaders I interviewed had career paths that were not smooth diagonal lines to a preconceived pinnacle. Instead, their career paths were defined by the number of times they took risks, accepting or seeking assignments that were outside their previously described area of expertise.

Leading his $3 billion company through three major crises – the U.S.-China trade war in 2018, the Missouri River flood in 2019, and COVID in 2020, all while taking care of his people and increasing revenue, Steve Kaniewski, President and CEO of Valmont Industries, is a perfect example of a champion leader who, guided by his C^2 Factor, took various twists and turns in his professional development. When I asked what accounted for his success, he told me:

> My drive came from curiosity. I started my career in direct marketing then moved to tech. I got 40,000 shares of nothing but learned a lot and got curious about systems and from there moved to ops. I was running a $400 million facility at 23-years-old making $26,000 but I knew I could parlay it into something else. You've got to have the courage to take opportunity when it presents itself, even when you don't feel like you're ready or it's the right time, or even if you feel intimidated. It doesn't matter if you fail if you learn.

"I wouldn't be where I am without curiosity leading the way. I started in tech and stayed in tech. But I started in marketing and followed my curious heart from one part of the business to another," Google executive Kelly Ducourty told me. She further added:

> While in marketing, I learned to think through the external lens, but I soon realized that I simply couldn't market something if I didn't really under-stand it. So, I stepped out of my comfort zone, hungry to earn some more technical knowledge. That's how I ended in the solution architecture group and started truly from scratch. While there were moments in which I was intimidated on the journey, my determination was stronger and kept me going. Day by day I learned more until one day I was the leading solution

architect in the company at that time. That serves as a reminder for me, even today, to never allow myself to become complacent. I strongly believe that there is nothing you can't learn or can't do if you approach it with the courage to leave something you master behind and with the curiosity and excitement to explore a different area that will take you further.

Ducourty is now the Vice President of GTM Strategy and Operations at Google.

Wendy Dean is the President and Co-founder of Moral Injury of Healthcare, an organization that combats the suffering that occurs when healthcare providers are "repeatedly expected, in the course of providing care, to make choices that transgress their long-standing, deeply-held commitment to healing" – talk about a courageous mission! The name of her umbrella organization is Relentlessly Curious, LLC. Clearly, a champion leader with a strong C² Factor, she talked to me about her zigzag career:

> Except for my surgical internship, I was never the obvious choice for a job because my training wasn't specific to the position. But, knowing how to adapt skills from previous positions, identifying and assimilating estab-lished knowledge in the new field, and relying on both the expertise around me and my own work ethic, I knew I could succeed.

It is easy to see how those zigzag career paths were enabled by their C² Factor – motivated at least in part by curiosity and enabled by courage.

Continual questioning: In addition to zigzagging career paths to combat settling into a too expert perspective, champion leaders ask difficult questions and welcome new information, even when it challenges their own ideas.

"I think one of the questions that is critical for all business decision-makers, yet is rarely asked, is 'why?' I think it is the core question of curiosity or inquisitiveness," former Cisco Consulting Services executive Jon Stine told me. "It explores potential root causes, which can be time consuming, but it can lead a project in a different direction. 'Why' is the question that has to be answered repeatedly and it takes remarkable courage," said Stine, now Executive Director of Open Voice Network.

Some questions like "why?" are simple to implement and are likely to have untold positive results, but remember I said some parts of engaging your C² Factor are simple, but not easy? Continual questioning and seeking information, particularly when it conflicts with your own views, is not easy. Obviously, it takes courage to ask people to challenge your ideas, but it's possible, even probable, that they simply won't do it.

When senior executives advocate for a certain approach, team members are often reluctant to challenge them. Too many times while shadowing leaders, I have sat through strategy sessions and witnessed silent responses in the group meeting followed by heated conversations between pairs in the hallways. A number of senior executives I've worked with say that even when they are not advocating, but merely suggesting, they have difficulty getting pushback on their ideas. This is a dangerous dynamic. In his book, *Why Great Leaders Don't Take Yes for an Answer*, Michael Roberto[2] describes the danger inherent in a "culture of yes" that occurs in many organizations. The danger is the same as if you as the leader made the decisions on your own.

Champion leaders recognize this danger and engage the C^2 Factor to insist that an idea is challenged, and flaws or additional opportunities are identified – because they do exist in any solution. They ask questions such as follows:

- What perspectives haven't I taken?
- Which stakeholders haven't I considered?
- Which functional expertise has not been included?
- What are the global and local implications?
- What are the short-term/long-term trade-offs?

The purpose isn't to find a perfect solution, but to recognize and account for as many implications as possible. John Chambers, the CEO of CISCO, is known to have often said: "Don't tell me what I'm doing right. Tell me what I'm doing wrong." No doubt that led to his success in steering his company through the technology collapse in 2000 and then growing the revenue to $40+ billion.

Champion leaders engage the C^2 Factor to search for outliers and facts that don't fit their vision of where to go and how to get there.

3. Too Fast

How many times have you been on the phone with a member of your leadership team as you drive to work, talking about an issue that appears to have such an easy answer, you wonder why someone else hasn't thought of it? You say something like, "This is a no-brainer, just go ahead and do...." Leaders are expected to make decisions and make them fast. Others are waiting for direction and there is pressure to act!

Have you ever ok'd a plan without really listening to the details because someone stopped you in the hallway as you were rushing to your next meeting? Most of us have taken a "ready ... don't bother to aim ... shoot" approach at some point without being curious about the details nor being courageous enough to resist the pull to respond immediately to a request for help.

The demand to take action can lead to oversimplification and a rush to judgment. There may be reasons why the obvious answer hasn't been applied. Simplifying is often lauded as a leadership skill, but that is in regard to communication, not strategic decision-making. Leaders must confront complex business and organizational concerns which require deep thinking that curiosity inspires. Think about the leaders you know who, without much C² Factor, tried to oversimplify issues such as healthcare. Their communication was reckless, their actual impact that of a robotic leader.

The Navy's handling of the problems that led up to the 2017 fatal collision between a U.S. Navy destroyer and a cargo ship exemplifies this kind of speedy oversimplification. Instead of engaging their C² Factor to delve deeply into the details, Navy leaders came up with a simple explanation for what had happened.

The Navy had been embroiled in another scandal seven years prior known as the "Fat Leonard" affair that involved a large contracting company. Apparently looking for a non-Navy scapegoat, they simply lumped the incident under that umbrella which was already "old news" so less likely to cause alarm.[3]

Champion leaders understand that all solutions can't be found in ten bullet points or the equivalent of the first page of a Google search. Especially on matters of great importance, they have the courage to insist on deep inquiry even though it inevitably takes time.

Increase your speed by slowing down: Given the enormous pressure to take action, pausing may seem counterintuitive. Champion leaders recognize the need to act but know that impulsive action is reckless and often results in costing the organization more time and damage than a well-thought-out plan.

The "Fat Leonard" scandal mentioned above refers to the 2013 arrest of Leonard Glenn Francis, the 350-pound owner of a support contracting company. For years, he had overcharged for his services and had bribed key decision-makers, contracting officers and Navy security officials to win contracts. Although corruption was known to be widespread, there have been very few indictments and even fewer convictions.

If Navy officials had engaged the C^2 Factor, they might have conducted a more in-depth investigation into a number of disturbing incidents, including the capture of patrol boats by Iranian forces in 2016; the 2017 fatal collision between a destroyer and a cargo ship; and the 2020 pierside fire that resulted in the total loss of a warship. If they had slowed down and had the courage to be curious, they might have discovered as the National Transportation Safety Board did in 2020 when they investigated, that the ship-handling accidents were related to a host of systemic naval problems and not vaguely somehow related to the "Fat Leonard" scandal There might have been more arrests, disciplinary actions, and changes in the system.

Now, in July 2021, the results of a survey requested by a group of Republican lawmakers and overseen by a retired Navy admiral and Marine general unveils that 94% of the sailors surveyed[4] reported that the damaging operational failures were related to Navy culture and leadership problems. One hopes that Navy leaders will finally slow down to engage in both curiosity and courage.

Champion leaders understand the necessity of slowing down despite the courage it takes to do so. They understand that this pause is essential to engaging the C^2 Factor which in turn enables creative thinking, accurate analysis, and then decisive action. Nearly all of the champions I interviewed espouse the benefits of establishing a built-in period of quiet, away from the demands of email, news feeds, well-meaning colleagues, and even family and friends, in order to have time for undisturbed reflection.

By slowing down, champion leaders have time to call upon what they have taken in because of their curiosity – the perspectives of their teams, stakeholders, the outside world. They center themselves, check their relationships, utilize their teams to challenge their thinking and round out ideas, and then use courage to take action. Champion leaders slow down in order to move forward with greater clarity, momentum, and impact.

One only need to think about leaders like Bill Gates to validate the value of this concept of slowing down. Bill Gates is famous for his "Think Weeks" during which time he isolated himself to reflect on the strategic direction of Microsoft. Another very successful, young CEO has also implemented this approach – Mark Zuckerberg.

ENGAGING THE C² FACTOR – AN IMPERATIVE FOR STRATEGIC THINKING

Popular and widely accepted research about strategic thinking comes from the Wharton School of the University of Pennsylvania and is referenced by an article in *Harvard Business Review*, 2013.[5] It involved over 20,000 executives and identified six skills that they concluded are essential to master and synchronously apply in order for leaders to think strategically. They include abilities to anticipate, challenge, interpret, decide, align, and learn. Although the C² Factor is inherent to each of these abilities, this section will focus predominantly on anticipate, challenge, and decide.

1. Anticipate

Robotic leaders are poor at detecting threats and opportunities on the periphery of their business. Academic leaders may anticipate events but never venture beyond theorizing about them, and reckless leaders may act without fully understanding the implications of perceived threats or opportunities. Champion leaders, in contrast, use the curiosity element of their C² Factor, keeping their ears open and their noses in the air, observing their environment and anticipating what changes might lie ahead.

Intel's Andy Grove[6] was just such a champion leader. He is famous for feeding his curiosity – and by default his well-rounded knowledge – with month-long sabbaticals during which he read extensively across a wide variety of topics and engaged in conversations with people outside his field. Andy had a kind of "T"-shaped curiosity – he was both a browser with curiosity about a broad range of topics and an expert in his field. This knowledge helped him anticipate change and successfully reinvent his company several times throughout its history.

Champion leaders I spoke with reiterated the need to "anticipate" by being aware. As Carlo Bertollati, former Deputy General Manager at Yves Rocher and current Marketing and Communications Director at Stanhome, Italy, told me, "You have to be curious not only about how you are doing and how the competition is doing, but also about other sectors, industries, and what is happening with them." Tien Wong, CEO at Opus8, a private investment and advisory firm, focused his remarks on anticipating need, "When working in an environment which is changing with lightning speed if you don't have adaptable teams you're in trouble. One way to stay adaptable is by constantly learning and being curious and figuring out where the next need is."

Champion leaders engage their curiosity element of their C^2 Factor and anticipate by actively observing their surroundings and questioning how what they see will impact their business. Jackie Sturm, Corporate Vice President of Global Supply Chain Operations at Intel Corporation, summarized it like this:

> Leaders are not here to take you where you were already going. We here to try to identify what's going on in the world and figure out how to forge a new path that supports the growth or the success of the organization. We need to be looking at the world from a different perspective. We need to be saying, "Hey, I know what my business looks like today. I know what the economy looks like today, but what am I sensing and learning from what's happening around me that will impact the future."

Champion leaders are willing to bet on their anticipation about how the world will look. "You put a stake in the ground and go," former McAfee executive, Patricia Hatter, told me. She emphasizes the importance of listening, gathering data points, synthesizing the information, and making the call about where the market is going. Our conversation prompted her to remember when she was at McAfee and began advocating for moving services to the cloud. The now-SVP Global Chief Customer Officer, Palo Alto Networks, said:

> It seems obvious now but at the time it sounded crazy. I believed that I was right and so at every opportunity I had, I would bring up the topic. In executive staff conversations somehow, I'd find a way to get to that topic.

Champion leaders engage their curiosity about a wide variety of topics, some seemingly unrelated to their businesses and absorb information through a variety of channels to ensure they do not live in an echo chamber surrounded by people in the same line of work, from the same social circle, or with the same political beliefs. One client of mine who lives in New York City makes a point of socializing with friends of her family when she visits them in the Midwest. "They read different books, listen to different music, and have different ideas about how to solve the world's problems. Sometimes it's hard to listen, but I almost always learn something."

2. Challenge

Questioning your own beliefs and the status quo is essential to exemplary strategic thinking, and champion leaders have the courage to do it. As Steve Kaniewski, CEO of Valmont Industries, told me, "You can't play follow the leader. You need to be contrarian, disruptive."

Nerissa Naidu is a seasoned board member and the CEO of FinTech, āxil, a Top 3 of Female Fintechs for 2020 company, has been in numerous senior executive roles where she has managed a 5,000+ global workforce and performed multinational strategic turnarounds in Fortune 100 companies. She put it this way: "For the sustainability of businesses, companies need to really be thinking about curiosity and have the courage to challenge what used to work and say, 'that approach doesn't work anymore.'"

Challenge refers not only to challenging yourself, but also being willing to challenge others, including those to whom one reports. Pablo Koziner, a former Caterpillar executive and the current President of Energy and Commercial at Nikola Motor Company, told me how he challenged his boss when he was first promoted to a new role. "My boss gave me a set of instructions and started to tell me everything that was wrong and what I needed to do to fix it." Pablo challenged his boss by asking for the opportunity to talk to the people in the areas where he thought the problems were. Pablo used courage to be able to exercise his curiosity and as a result found very different problems than the ones his boss had identified.

3. Decide

Champion strategic thinkers, relying on their curiosity, insist on developing multiple options for the path forward. They then call on their courage to make tough calls, often with incomplete information. In uncertain times, champion leaders follow a disciplined process that considers the trade-offs involved and take both short- and long-term goals into account. They take calculated risks. It is easy to overlook the importance of this skill and the courage it takes to execute. Because the decisions champion leaders make are based on the curiosity-informed anticipation of the future – changes in technology, consumer demands, sociopolitical conditions, etc. – it makes these decisions look simple in retrospect. At the time, however, they were decisions that involved substantial risk and, therefore, courage.

Examples[7] abound:

- In 1999, when Zappos was struggling, founder Nick Swinmurn decided to offer free shipping and returns.
- In the 2008 financial crisis, Ford's Alan Mulally refused government bailout money and borrowed $23.5 billion, avoided bankruptcy, regained market share, and ultimately returned the car maker to profitability.
- Named CEO of PepsiCo in 2006, Indra Nooyi foresaw the coming shift among consumers to healthier foods and beverages and immediately introduced PepsiCo's strategy to respond. In 2013, when PepsiCo was challenged by activist Peltz to split the company, Nooyi steadfastly refused. Instead, she restructured her leadership team to continue delivering strong performance.
- Reed Hastings, co-founder and CEO of Netflix, pivoted a no-late-fees, no-due-dates DVD subscription service into an online streaming product. In retrospect, that seem like it was a "no-brainer," but it was not clear at the time how streaming would come to dominate.

Figure 6.2 reminds us how the alchemy of curiosity and courage leads to better decisions-making, especially in the face of some kind of threat.

Champion leaders make courageous decisions informed by processes that involved convergent thinking informed by curiosity. Pablo Koziner, the senior executive at Nikola Motor Company, described his process to me:

> Great leaders don't play it safe. They don't just try to improve incre-mentally, they push, innovate, drive great value and that takes a lot of courage.
>
> I'm someone that has to take risk in my role. I make decisions where the outcome is very uncertain. I ultimately must rest those decisions on some fundamental information, so I ask myself:
>
> - Did you work hard to be well-informed?
> - Did you consult with people?
> - Did you listen effectively?
> - Are you doing these things for the right reasons?
> - Is this action best for the company or is this for a career advancement opportunity?

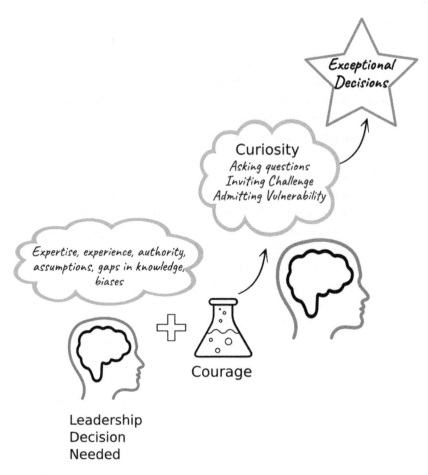

FIGURE 6.2
The C² Factor in decision-making.

- Do you have the humility to understand that this could be wrong, and have you taken the time to vet this?

If I can answer yes to all those questions, I move forward. That's the way I handle decisions and empower courage.

4. Interpret, Align, and Learn

Interpret: As previously discussed, champion leaders intentionally and consciously slow down and step back to do the critical thinking necessary in crafting strategy. They pause to think more deeply and to remain curious about what they know and don't know, recognizing that data is not the same as knowledge and knowledge is not the same as wisdom.

Because champion leaders also ask challenging questions and invite disparate points of view, inevitably they receive complex and often conflicting information. They take the time to synthesize the input, looking for patterns and new insights. Rather than disregarding "outliers," champion leaders take time to reflect on the apparent contradictions. They look for higher order themes that can inform strategic solutions. The Wharton research refers to this as "interpreting."

Align: Strategic alignment means that the organization's culture, structure, and use of resources support the organizations' strategy. Similarly, all business units and employees work in concert with strategic goals.

As mentioned, champion leaders seek out disparate points of view and invite communication. This is a critical step in achieving alignment. Frequent interaction, not just "all hands" meetings but one-on-one meetings, is a key way in which a leader demonstrates true curiosity about others' perspectives on issues and builds trust. Having the courage to hear and respond to concerns helps attain alignment.

Learn: It goes without saying, champion leaders who by definition have high C^2 Factor place a high value on continuous learning, not only for themselves but also for their whole organization. And although they do like to read and support formal training in their employees, the champion leader is more interested in learning through experience both on and off the job. Champion leaders create a culture in which inquiry is valued and mistakes are viewed as learning opportunities by modeling the C^2 Factor in approaching their own failures. They encourage exploring both successful and unsuccessful initiatives not to assign blame but to look for the lessons that can be learned. And they have the courage to communicate the findings to employees so that they can learn.

5. The Strategy Landscape

A Google search of "organizational strategy" produces 231 million results in 0.72 seconds. A search for "innovation strategy" produces 1.78 billion in 0.58 seconds. Clearly, there is money to be made providing "the next best thing." Business leaders can be susceptible to embracing the latest solution whether it's Six-Sigma, Blue Ocean Strategy, Lean Six-Sigma, the color of leadership, DISC types, or any other model. One executive half-jokingly remarked to me, "we all dread it when the chairman goes to a conference because we know he will be excited about the next new trend in strategy." Champion leaders view methodology through the lens of the C² Factor. They have curiosity about what the methodology has to offer but also about the underlying assumptions that any one method applies to their organization or to their current situation. They have the courage to experiment but also challenge any particular approach.

Organizational agility is one of the concepts that has dominated the strategy landscape for the last two decades. The concept of agility originated in the software world over two decades ago and refers to ability of an organization to adapt, change quickly, and succeed in a rapidly changing, ambiguous environment. It calls for small multidisciplinary teams that focus on delivering results in a fast, experimental, and iterative manner.

Designed to respond to the changing needs of customers, agility is seen as a quicker way of bringing incremental innovations and new products/services to the market. The role of senior leaders in agile organizations is to provide strategic guidance around priorities and expected outcomes. *Forbes*[8] magazine lists 15 key qualities that define agile leaders: being open, accepting and present, collaborating, comfortable with being uncomfortable, always listening, learning continuously, able to deal with frequent disruption, curious, self-aware, creating inclusive and empowered teams, leading by example, cooperating courageously, adaptive, and flexible. Note how many of these are directly or indirectly elements of the C² Factor.

Having looked at how champion leaders eschew business as usual to be able to utilize their C² Factor and engage in strategic thinking, we can now turn to the impact of such leadership on their organizations and how to establish and sustain a culture of curiosity and courage.

NOTES

1. https://en.wikipedia.org/wiki/Richard_Branson.
2. Roberto, Michael. "Why Great Leaders Don't Take Yes for an Answer." Wharton School Publishing, June 10, 2005. https://wsp.wharton.upenn.edu/.
3. Hooper, Craig. "As Investigators ID Big Problems, US Navy Blames "Fat Leonard"." *Forbes*, September 4, 2020.
4. https://news.usni.org/2021/07/12/lawmakers-survey-94-of-sailors-say-damaging-operational-failures-related-to-navy-culture-leadership-problems.

5. Shoemaker, Paul J.H., Krupp, Steve, and Howland, Samantha. "Strategic Leadership: The Essential Skills." *Harvard Business Review*, January–February 2013.
6. Grove, Andy. *Only the Paranoid Survive: How to Exploit the Crisis Points that Challenge Every Company*. New York: Doubleday Business; 1st edition (1996).
7. Harnish, Verne, Collins, Jim, and editors of Fortune. *The Greatest Business Decisions of All Time: How Apple, Ford, IBM, Zappos, and Others Made Radical Choices that Changed the Course of Business*. Time Home Entertainment; 1st edition (October 2, 2012).
8. https://www.forbes.com/sites/forbescoachescouncil/2020/06/17/15-key-qualities -that-define-an-agile-leader/.

7

Ensuring Prosperity with a C² Factor Culture

Beyond any one individual leader, the C² Factor must be woven into the cultural fabric of an organization to make meaningful impact. Champion leaders recognize that curiosity is ignited and sustained by an organizational culture that values diversity of thought, supports reasonable risks, does not punish mistakes, and invites courageousness. They know a culture that promotes the C² Factor starts at the top as senior leaders model desired behaviors and values. But some aspects of corporate culture are hindrances to the expression of curiosity and courage, creating negative consequences for the organization. How do we avoid those obstacles? What are key practices for creating and sustaining the C² Factor and a subsequent culture of innovation and an organization prepared to welcome the future?

What if only you had the C² Factor? Can you imagine trying to inspire a workforce that was only interested in repeating what they've always done? Or execute a strategy with a leadership team that was only interested in talking about possibilities but would never commit to action? Or leading a group of division chiefs in a newly merged company who believed they knew all about your customers and services and were busy cutting personnel? Such would be the case if your workforce were full of robotic managers, your leadership team were like academics, and your new division chiefs were reckless leaders.

To make a meaningful impact, the C² Factor must expand beyond any one leader and be woven into the cultural fabric of the organization. Champion leaders recognize that curiosity is ignited and sustained by an organizational culture that values diversity of thought, supports taking

DOI: 10.4324/9781003212881-7

reasonable risks, does not punish mistakes, and invites courageousness. A culture that promotes the C² Factor begins at the top as senior leaders model the desired behavior and values.

Although the phrase "culture of continuous improvement" may sound desirable, it is far from adequate to meet the needs of organizations looking to embrace the future and thrive. Too often "continuous improvement" means small modifications of existing products, cutting costs, increasing the margins around existing services. Changes such as these though frequently painful for those who have to execute them are nonetheless simple to make.

For organizations to thrive, they need a culture of curiosity and courage, looking for new opportunities, asking new questions, and initiating change. The C² Factor culture is one of continuous innovation and champion leaders know that innovation must be understood to be the purview of the entire organization and not limited to the Innovation Department or research and development (R&D). They know that to have a thriving organization, each division and department, each level of responsibility must exercise curiosity and courage within their domain.

I am not suggesting that all elements of the C² Factor should be activated in all situations at all times. In fact, many of the champion leaders I interviewed, while extolling curiosity and courage as essential, underscored the importance of having "guardrails."

Cara Lessor, who founded an organization that uses the power of play to cultivate the creativity, curiosity, and compassion necessary to build healthier, more successful communities, said:

> You need to create a structure for curiosity and courage to actually happen. It needs to be purposeful and aligned with the organization's strategy. You need to operate within a framework so it's not just about, "Oh, let's imagine these things.".

The importance of the C² Factor and aligning it with the organization's goals is not limited to art, education, or creative companies. Industries that are inherently conservative also need a C² Factor that is within the guardrails of the mission.

John DiStasio was an executive of a power company of 2,100 employees during the energy crisis of 2000. The expectation at the time was that all utilities would lose their status as monopolies and these companies were in no position to be competitive. As he described it, these companies were used to coping with glacial movements in the market and in 2000, they were facing "slush."

> It was very important to have the curiosity and courage to stop asking the same questions and getting the same answers, because frankly that's where we already were, and we needed incentive to change. We needed the courage to challenge our own status quo and think about things differently.

John knew he needed the C^2 Factor, and he also knew that he needed "guardrails" to ensure alignment with the organization's mission. Within those guardrails, he provided freedom for people to take risks and to be curious, and to be courageous.

Much like the individual leaders' constraints that we explored in the previous chapter, organizations often have constraints that inhibit individuals from engaging their C^2 Factor, including the sheer size of the organization, administrative hierarchies, and the natural conservatism of some industries. It takes conscious effort to address these potential inhibitors with structure, policies, and processes that enable the C^2 Factor to flourish.

CONFRONTING CORPORATE CONSTRAINTS

Corporate constraints both cause the inhibition of the C^2 Factor and are the result of that inhibition. This negative feedback loop weakens the performance of the organization in the present and undermines its capacity to anticipate and thrive in the future.

1. Too Successful

A focus on innovation is a common value espoused by organizations, but that means "change" and change is hard, especially when one has been successful. In a transforming world, it is not enough to improve incrementally. Mary Jane Raymond, the CFO of II-VI, Inc., believes when a company becomes overly attached to a successful idea, product, or service, curiosity gets shut down and the company stops paying attention to changing conditions. "They just get way overconfident and it's that overconfidence that ultimately brings companies down," she says.

Andy Grove, CEO of Intel, was well aware of this phenomenon as he famously asserted "Success breeds complacency. Complacency breeds failure. Only the paranoid survive." Yet following his departure, Intel, "the firm that did more than perhaps any other to put the 'silicon' in Silicon Valley," has fallen victim to the dangers of success. Its manufacturing technology has fallen behind and some of its big customers such as Apple and Amazon are turning into competitors. As of this date, Intel remains a leader in the chip market, but it is struggling to meet present demands and prepare for the future.[1,2]

Even start-ups are not immune to a diminishing C² Factor as they become successful. "I've experienced companies that exhibited great courage and creativity early on and achieved success, but here's what went wrong: They didn't have the courage for creative destruction. They became comfortable with their success and relied on it. They ossified," said David Giannini, an executive with more than 20 years' experience in building enterprises that capitalize on emerging technologies, converging economies, and disruptive business models.

Champion leaders combat complacency with the C² Factor. David went on, "When you've achieved success and everybody is telling you how smart you are, it's really easy to just fall back on that success. That's when you really need courage and curiosity. You've got to get out of your comfort zone."

Successful companies grow and with size, there comes an inevitable need to get organized. It doesn't make sense to reinvent the wheel for every situation that presents itself and there is reason to want to have a consistent product or service that reflects the quality behind the organization's brand. But with standardization can come inhibitors to the C² Factor and the health of the company.

2. Too Standardized

Imrana Jalal, a Fijian lawyer and an International Human Rights lawyer, is Chair of the Inspection Panel of the World Bank. The Inspection Panel is the World Bank's international accountability mechanism which investigates complaints against the Bank's projects and investments in the developing world, a mission requiring high levels of the C² Factor. Her team goes into extremely rural areas such as the Amazon jungle and the

Nile River, often under threats of intimidation and reprisals, to gather information on the negative impact the World Bank's activities may have had on the local area.

Even though the Inspection Panel is accountable only to the board, she still struggles with creating space for her team's C² Factor:

> I have to allow flexibility of thinking and big institutions are not good at that. They need to welcome innovation. They need to say, if you're curious about this issue expand it, but because of the hierarchical nature of huge institutions, it's almost antithetical to their character.

Implicit in a hierarchical structure in which the roles are tightly delineated is a command-and-control mindset that can inhibit the C² Factor and its concomitant contribution to growth and sustainability of a business. A former Cisco executive told me about a time when a new set of senior leaders were brought into the company, "They didn't want courage. They wanted obedience. They wanted everyone to toe the line because it minimized risk for them. But it also limited their growth. Their results were much smaller than their potential," she said.

However, simply eliminating the hierarchies is not necessarily the answer. Matrixed organizations, popularized by the interest in having agile organizations, have their limitations as well. Progress can be bogged down by seemingly countless meetings. Gaining buy-in from so many stakeholders can result in a lot of doing, but not a lot of accomplishing. It can be a kind of tyranny of consensus.

Meetings and emphasis on team decisions in practice can result in no one taking responsibility for decisions. It takes curiosity to examine whether these structures are accomplishing what they intend to, what elements of the structure works and what elements do not, and in which departments one structure might be preferable over another.

Challenging structure may not be enough. To really engage the C² Factor, one can't be fooled by the kind of "restructuring" that throws all the pieces up in the air, but the culture remains the same.

Almost as risky as challenging the organization's structure is challenging so-called best practices that are embedded in an organization. Several champion leaders I spoke with talked about how curiosity was stifled when they inherited teams that seemed to be invested in maintaining the status quo. We've all heard the refrains, "we've always done it this way'" and "that won't work here." In these situations, as long as they don't rock the boat, poor decisions are made.

I worked with one leader who advocated for a merger deal even though she knew it was not good for the company because she knew that senior stakeholders liked the idea. It didn't rock the boat, so it was acceptable despite its inadequacies. Clearly, she was not a champion leader. As Warren Buffet[3] once said, "As a group, lemmings may have a rotten image, but no individual lemming has ever received bad press."

3. Too Focused (on the wrong things)

Organizations diminish their capacity to engage the C² Factor when they lose sight of their mission, their *raison d'être*. Whether it's to entertain, inform and inspire people, promote world peace, empower people with technology, cure cancer or make widgets that improve peoples' lives, when organizations forget about their "why" and focus on the "how," they have undoubtedly lost the capacity to take advantage of the C² Factor and will continue to do so. Focusing on the wrong things is worse than not focusing at all.

One example is the overfocus on quarterly numbers. Former Cisco senior executive Dick Cantwell related:

> Without curiosity, courage in leadership, we'd continue to embrace the status quo which leads to just incremental results and a loss of competitive advantage. Innovation is the key to growth and the biggest inhibitor is the need to deliver short term results, which are easier to do by continuing to drive the status quo.

Or, as another former senior executive at a Fortune 500 company told me: "They want you to be creative, but only after you've made your numbers."

Money can also be used as an excuse to not pursue new ideas. It's easy to hide behind "they'd never approve budget for that" or "I'm sorry but that's just not in the budget." Whether you are an individual contributor with a new idea, the department head, general manager of a business unit, or in the C-suite, there are lots of ways to use money to suppress the C² Factor. Money is often a legitimate constraint, but I was surprised by the number of CFOs I interviewed who thought that money was used to cut off exploration of new initiatives. Mary Jane Raymond, the CFO from II-VI, for example, told me how surprised she was by peoples' reluctance to ask for what she considered a relatively small amount of money to explore innovative projects.

An emphasis on process over product also inhibits the C² Factor. Wendy Dean, a physician and Medical Officer at an Army research enterprise said:

> When leaders are overly controlling; when they are more focused on the right process than the right outcome, they don't tap people's full potential and they lose opportunities to progress. Regulated industries, such as utilities and healthcare, may suffer from a lack of the C² Factor if their regulators fail to be curious about the impact of their rules or to be courageous enough to challenge the legitimacy of them.

It takes the C² Factor to concentrate on the customer. An executive from Silicon Valley who asked not to be identified declared, "Despite the fact that many companies claim to be customer centric, it takes courage to represent the customer's interests within a large organization." He went on to tell me about a situation in which the general manager of a business unit refused to do research, listen to differing opinions, or explore the marketplace for a product in which he was invested. The general manager insisted that the product be brought to market, even though it was neither well-developed nor differentiated enough to be competitive. This executive I spoke to declared, "it takes great courage to ask yourself if your loyalty lies with the organization serving the customer or with the individual who holds the purse strings for your job and your compensation."

When Judge Bobbie McCartney became Chief Judge of the New Orleans Social Security Hearing Office, she had to ask where the organization's loyalties lay. And is that what the office focus should be? When she joined the office, performance was ranked at the bottom of the 140 offices in the country. It had a backlog of over 2,000 pending cases. Judge McCartney investigated and found that there were no incentives for cases to be resolved, no repercussions for low productivity, and a cadre of private sector attorneys benefiting from cases being delayed. The staff was overwhelmed and hopeless about changing.

Judge McCartney knew she had to energize the staff and confront some of the well-established practices impeding services. To motivate the staff, she set out to engage their curiosity:

> During meetings I would pick a file from the backlog and bring it to life. I'd say, "this is a child who lives in our neighborhood and is completely

disabled. He has been waiting a year and a half for us to look at his case. In the meantime, he cannot qualify for necessary lifesaving surgeries or medical assistance. A year and a half in the life of a child – from six to seven and a half – without the proper medical treatment." I got the staff curious about the lives behind these cases and they came to life.

Relying on courage, Judge McCartney involved the local bar association to look at the patterns of practice of some attorneys benefiting from the backlog and enlisted local congressmen to help get additional resources, bringing in additional judges from across the country to help:

> We disposed of an average of 600 cases each month for three months with this highly focused initiative, each judge averaging about a hundred cases, taking a huge bite out of the backlog. Working together, the New Orleans office went from the bottom at 140 to the top 12 in a year's time.

A champion leader, Judge McCartney used curiosity and courage to get the focus back onto the customer where it belongs.

ESTABLISHED, FOSTERED, AND SUSTAINED THROUGH CONSCIOUS COMMITMENT

There is a famous Peter Drucker saying, "culture eats strategy for breakfast." He meant that no matter how good your strategy is, it will not be successful if you have the wrong people and the wrong culture. Champion leaders know that a culture based on the C² Factor has employees who are engaged and who will execute strategy that meets present demands and is geared for the future. It means that curiosity and courage are part of everyday life in the organization and not a separate activity in the "innovation department."

Nerissa Naidu is an example of a leader who knows how to create such a culture. As someone who has led innovation initiatives, Nerissa knows that innovation can't be left to one department. As she told me, "Too often people will say 'we have a group that deals with that, so everyone else just do your daily jobs.'" Naidu knows that innovation needs to be spread across the entire organization. "Curiosity is not a department and courage is not an HR thing."

Tien Wong, the CEO of a private investment firm, gave me a great example of how when the C² Factor is cascaded throughout the organization, it pays off. His team was working for a Fortune 100 company doing technical support work when someone noticed an unusual pattern. They became curious about why the pattern was there. They dug deeper into the situation and discovered widespread fraud.

Tien described telling their customer what they had discovered:

> You have to be courageous to bring up a situation like that. The customer doesn't want to know that fraud is being committed and they didn't detect it. It's a difficult conversation. But we ended up developing new technology and a new service around fraud detection for us and saved the customer money. That was all because one person doing their job being curious and courageous.

Before you begin efforts to build a C² culture, first, a warning based on a 2018 article in *Harvard Business Review*.[4] Even when you are mindful of trying to build a culture of curiosity and courage, you need to pause and be curious about your assumptions and what you might be missing.

The authors surveyed 16,000 employees and over 1,500 C-suite leaders across industries and at various levels of leadership to understand how they view the role of curiosity at their organizations. Of the most senior executives, 83% reported that curiosity is encouraged "a great deal" or "a good amount" at their company, but only 52% of individual contributors said the same. About half (49%) of those same executives reported that curiosity is rewarded by salary growth, but only 16% of individual contributors agreed. Champion leaders must be curious about how curiosity and courage actually manifest in their organizations and be courageous enough to confront potential gaps between their perceptions and reality.

So how does one create such a culture? Creating a culture requires a conscious commitment to and focus on the desired values. Leaders must reflect the value they place on the C² Factor by (1) who they hire, (2) how they enable the C² Factor, (3) how they reward the C² Factor, and (4) how they model, mentor, and sponsor the C² Factor for others.

1. Hiring

The well-known author of *Good to Great* and many other books on business, Jim Collins[5] echoes Peter Drucker's emphasis on having the right people. He asserts that hiring the right people is essential for creating a great company, that when the right people are hired, the company is prepared to adapt to the changing world, that the company moves in the right direction, and that managing and motivating employees is not a problem.

Screening applicants: To foster the C² Factor in their organizations, champion leaders screen their applicants with this in mind. Many of the executives I interviewed explicitly look for candidates who are curious and courageous when they are recruiting and hiring.

Intel's Julie Coppernoll, Corporate Vice President of Global Marketing Strategy relayed:

> One of the best ways to identify someone with those qualities in an interview is by the kind of questions they ask you. The second way is to look at what they've done in their life, their career and how they approach new things.

Nani Coloretti, Senior Vice President for Business and Financial Strategy at the Urban Institute, told me that she looks for curiosity and courage when she asks candidates to tell her about a time when they worked really hard on a project, and it did not go well. "Standing tall in the face of failure and taking responsibility for it takes courage and it also takes curiosity to understand what happened and what they learned."

Gary Kapusta, COO at II-VI, said: We can always find people that have the right skill sets. The real challenge is getting people that can think outside the box and challenge the status quo. Courage and curiosity are required to challenge people that have years or maybe decades more experience."

Champion leaders prefer being around other people with a high C² Factor. "I look for the people who demonstrate curiosity, the people who like to keep up with what's happening in the world and comments on those things tend to be also just more fun to work with. They feel engaged," former Capital One SVP Meredith Fuchs told me. Fuchs is now General Counsel for Plaid.

Seeking diversity: When asked how to cultivate a C² Factor culture, 100% of the leaders interviewed identified diversity as key. Champion leaders insist on having a diverse workforce at all levels of the organization.

The default way to think about diversity is often in terms of racial and gender differences which are, indeed, important, but in addition to being a morally laudable endeavor, why should organizations care about diversity? It is not about the color of one's skin, the language one speaks, or which rest room one uses. These differences bring with them distinctive lived experiences and therefore diverse ways of thinking, different values, varied preferences, and approaches to obstacles and opportunities.

The concept of diversity can be broadened to include generational differences, differences in education, professional background, expertise and training. Julie Coppernoll, a corporate VP at Intel, suggested even socio-economic background might be worth considering. These champion leaders want this diversity because they know that it leads to better problem-solving and creative thinking. Jackie Sturm, also a senior executive at Intel, confirmed the importance of diversity: "New thinking comes from having a diverse team where people look at the world from different angles. It gives you a better answer."

In addition, there are other forms of diversity that champion leaders consider important – professional discipline, personality, and work style, for example. And it is not sufficient to merely have diversity; to reap diversity's benefits, we have to celebrate those differences. Ana Pinczuk, the Chief Development Officer at Anaplan, shared with me an example of a way she put diversity to work. She hired someone from IBM who she described as "sort of a combination illustrator and architect" and told him to ignore their approach to building products and take some time to "ideate about how to build more composable products." She expected him to come up with one idea; instead, he came back with nine!

What interested her the most, however, was the impact his presentation had on the team. "It was quite freeing. He had such a wide gamut of ideas it spawned curiosity in other people." One of those ideas opened a whole new area of products. "It's a pretty big idea that would have never happened if we just kept the same old approach." If the leader has courage to embrace the possibilities inherent in diversity, it generates curiosity and with additional courage, leads to innovation.

2. Enabling

Champion leaders enable the C² Factor in the leaders they manage by encouraging them to be continuously learning and to have courage in making decisions. Jackie Reed, the first non-family member to be CEO of a chain of 13 restaurants in Hawaii, told me that she embraced the idea that CEO stands for "chief enabling officer" adding, "I am proud to say that I have unleashed the sense of curiosity in the company."

Limiting the guard rails: Regarding those organizational guard rails mentioned previously, champion leaders recognize that boundaries should not be about constraint, but instead define mission-aligned areas where there can be exploration, innovation, and change. They are curious about the talent of their people and see themselves, as Jackie Reed expressed it, "the remover of obstacles."

Jim Autry turned around *Better Homes and Gardens* magazine when it was on the skids in 1962 and went on to become a senior executive at its parent company, Meredith Corporation.[6] At the time of his retirement in 1991, he was regarded as one of the most successful and respected magazine publishing executives in the United States. Autry cautions leaders about having too tight restraints on your people.

When asked how he was able to invigorate a business that was floundering, he said: "I kept watching bad management do it wrong. I decided I was going to change it by trusting people, by being curious about what they could do, and by having the courage to take the harnesses off people." Jim instituted some radical change management, which included energizing the staff by encouraging courage and curiosity. Jim described it as a balancing act. "You don't want guard rails to become such instruments of prohibition that they inhibit creativity. That is the balancing act that leaders have to do."

Allocating time and resources: Although champion leaders recognize that the C² Factor needs to be a part of everyday life for everyone, they also recognize that to extract the value of ideas and to try new things requires time and resources that are not earmarked for other activities. It's not that there must be a budget for the C² Factor, although that might not be a bad practice. Leaders must not be so demanding that their people are so busy that they have no time to observe their surroundings, reflect on their observations, or question assumptions underlying their work. In other words, to engage their curiosity. And when approached by staff with new ideas, leaders must be flexible enough to consider providing resources to explore their application. It requires courage for the staff to present these thoughts and courage for the leader to take steps to put ideas into action.

Ana Pinczuk, Chief Development Officer at Anaplan, was also a senior executive at Cisco where she had success running multimillion-dollar

P&Ls and led the transformation of Cisco's Global Technical Center. She spoke about how she grew the C² Factor in her organization.

> It's very basic. Just make time for it. You have to over-resource a little bit to allow enough time for people to get curious. We have to be careful to not squash that curiosity. We have to create time, space, and resources to allow folks to think differently in normal day-to-day work.

To that I would add a safe forum for asking questions, sharing and pitching new ideas.

3. Rewarding

Champion leaders know that behavior is shaped by what is rewarded, so they consciously reward instances of curiosity and courage and expect leaders throughout the organization to do the same. Performance reviews and promotions are based in part on a willingness to speak up, ask tough questions, and take risks. But it is not just formal rewards that count. Encouragement, recognition, and appreciation also are ways of rewarding the C² Factor.

When John DiStasio was CEO of the Sacramento Municipal Utility District, they had an ethic around innovation, ingenuity, and community:

> If people did something that demonstrated ingenuity, courage, creativity, or benefit to the community, we would recognize that. If you say you care about something, you've got to have a way to reinforce the behavior when you see it. You have to acknowledge it.

For speaking up: Meredith Fuchs, the General Counsel at Plaid, sees the willingness to take risk and put oneself out there as essential if one aspires to be a leader, so she actively encourages individuals to speak up. She has modeled curiosity and courage her whole career. First as a law clerk when she repeatedly challenged the judge to try to understand his reasoning, then as a young associate at a law firm where she "acted like a partner," confronting bad behavior she witnessed, and later when she took a risk to turn down a partnership offer to explore running a nonprofit. She calls upon these examples when she advises her leaders to demonstrate the C² Factor themselves and expect it from their teams.

Mary Jane Raymond, CFO from II-VI Inc., feels passionately about speaking up. Part of how she evaluates her team is based on their intellectual curiosity which she sees as manifested by asking the questions that need to be asked. "It is very important to raise your concerns. You cannot say no one asked me what I thought. At some point in your career, that's not even a cop out; it's a dismissible offense."

Champion leaders reward ideas even when they don't agree or think their ideas are unrealistic. Ana Pinczuk from Anaplan again:

> I think there's an element of allowing people to be ridiculous. I think part of curiosity is not shutting down bad ideas or things that aren't going to work. And that takes a lot of courage. It takes courage for the individual presenting, and it takes courage for the organization. You have to create an environment where people recover from a failure. They were curious; they went off and did something, boy, that thing stunk, but you learned something.

For taking a risk/trying: Interestingly enough, most leaders talked about not penalizing people who take risks. I can only assume that when one takes a risk that results in success, it is amply rewarded, but what about the times when things do not work out? Champion leaders know that at a very minimum, one should not be penalized for trying.

After 26 years at Intel, Elizabeth Eby is the CFO at the start-up, NeoPhotonics Inc. She wants to ensure that an entrepreneurial spirit of courage and curiosity are maintained as the organization grows:

> What I'm trying to figure out is how to make sure we don't lose that spirit going forward. I need to make sure there's no reprisals for taking risks, because I've seen that in organizations. Results orientation is balanced with the ability to let someone go off and try something new.

Gary Kapusta and Mary Jane Raymond of Intel both emphasized the importance of trying new things, even ones that failed in the past. Mary Jane:

> There is really a lot to be said for trying. I think leaders have to guide and upcoming leaders have to have a concept of trying. My view is that starting is everything. Even if you don't have a perfect timeline, just start. Lots of the things that are working today were seen as positively impossible and failed many times before.

Implied in these examples is the importance of psychological safety in enabling the C² Factor. In a psychologically safe space, people feel that they can share their thoughts and ideas without being penalized or humiliated. They trust that there is mutual respect for each other's competence.

Jackie Sturm, Intel's Corporate VP of Global Supply Chain Operations, who lead the charge for ensuring responsibly sourced minerals in Intel's microprocessors, worked for another well-known Silicon Valley icon, Apple, in its nascent days. She told me what happens when there is no psychological safety and how it suppresses curiosity and courage, ultimately resulting in the loss of both talent and opportunity for the company.

At the time, Jackie was the financial controller for the software organization at Apple. They had spent four years defining a system and she wanted the senior executives to provide resources for the next step. However, the executive management team was focused on maximizing their margin relative to the physical hardware and had no interest (curiosity) in what she had to say.

> People were starting to look at me like, "does she not get it?" It was really unsettling. It really quells your enthusiasm and your willingness to step up if you feel like every time I step up, people look at me like 'what's wrong with her?' At the time, it was not a psychologically safe environment. Even somebody who is really passionate will move on if they feel like they are talking to a brick wall and their reputation is being affected. We lost a huge amount of talent and the company really suffered.

Despite the courage demonstrated in repeatedly bringing up a new idea, the management team showed no curiosity. Perhaps individuals did have curiosity, but no courage, so the attitude of the CEO prevailed. When leadership changed and Steve Jobs returned, the company adopted the software strategy Jackie and others promoted and has since soared.

4. Modeling, Mentoring, and Sponsoring

Champion leaders understand that their attitude is absorbed by those around them, both indirectly and directly through modeling, mentoring, and sponsoring. They know that if they espouse values but then don't hold themselves accountable to lead in that fashion, their words become hollow.

Culture is established by the observed behavior of leaders, so modeling the C^2 Factor is crucial.

YY Lee models curiosity at Anaplan by publishing her cell phone number on Slack and encouraging all employees to reach out to her because "I'm super interested in what people have run across and what they observe." She talks to all incoming employees about strategy and what she's seeing in the market and especially because they have come from the outside, she urges them to share their reactions.

The one-on-one relationship in mentoring offers an excellent opportunity to help foster the C^2 Factor. As an experienced, trusted guide, the mentor provides advice and support in addition to role modeling. Julie Coppernoll challenges her leaders to ask questions and to consistently demonstrate that they want to understand and "that they're expecting their leaders to understand and to think in multiple dimensions. It's curiosity about the future, the markets, competitors and their success."

Having modeled and mentored others to engage their C^2 Factor, champion leaders understand that to make it safe to curiously explore and, especially, to take courageous action, leaders need to do more. They need to be sponsors. Modeling and mentoring are worthwhile, but when leaders are sponsors, they provide a level of safety that allows others to take courageous action.

When champion leaders are given opportunities for significantly challenging stretch assignments, they have the confidence that they can figure them out by using their curiosity, but they also credit the sponsorship of those leaders more senior to them who "had their back." To have a culture in which it is safe to demonstrate the C^2 Factor, we need leaders like YY Lee who put it this way, "the nature of leadership is about forging a path, rather than just executing the effort. And oftentimes forging a path means you stick your neck out so that the 400 people behind you don't have to stick their necks out."

We have seen how the C^2 Factor is important in enhancing one's satisfaction in life and one's effectiveness as a leader. We have looked at it at an individual level, a relationship level, a team level, and an organizational level. What would it mean if we applied curiosity and courage to how we approach the world?

NOTES

1. Seitz, Patrick. "Is Intel Stock a Buy after Chipmaker's Second-Quarter Earnings Report?" April 11, 2021. https://www.investors.com/news/technology/intel-stock-is-it-buy-now/.
2. Gelsinger, Pat. "Can Intel's New Boss Turn the Chipmaker Around?" *The Economist*, February 16, 2021.
3. https://buffettquotes.com/lemmings.
4. Harrison, Spencer, Pinkus, Erin, and Cohen, Jon, "Research: 83% of Executives Say They Encourage Curiosity. Just 52% of Employees Agree." *Harvard Business Review*, September 20, 2018.
5. Collins, Jim. *Good to Great: Why Some Companies Make the Leap and Others Don't.* New York: Harper Business; 1st edition, 2001.
6. Meredith Corporation owns magazines, television stations, websites, and radio stations with a readership of more than 120 million, paid circulation of more than 40 million, with websites that have nearly 135 million monthly unique visitors. Meredith's broadcast television stations reach 11% of U.S. households.

8

The Astounding Potential of Omnipresent C²

What happens if we apply the C² Factor to world problems? If the C² Factor has a profound effect on individual leaders, partners, teams, and corporate cultures, what could the impact be if it was applied to humanitarian challenges, social causes, or environmental issues? If we show up to every minute of our lives with the mindset of C², the world becomes a place with imminently more potential for change. Stories of two curious and courageous leaders will show us how clearly showing up with our C² Factor engaged can help make the world a better place. The blending of social mission with a viable business found in social entrepreneurism is an arena in which curiosity and courage are especially called for.

What would life be like if when we listened to the news, talked with our kids, overheard conversations in airports, had time to kill while waiting for an appointment, we engaged our C² Factor? What if when we saw someone doing something that seemed crazy to us or heard an opinion with which we vehemently disagreed, our first reaction was to be curious? What if when we saw an injustice, a misalignment of words and deeds, a person in distress our first thought was how we could do something about it? When we approach every situation with our C² Factor readily accessible, life is more interesting and satisfying, and we are more effective – as parents, partners, leaders, and citizens.

If political leaders could move along the curiosity and courage alchemy model represented by the infinity sign, sometimes showing up more curious and sometimes more courageous, but always with both available, would we be able to find peace and work together to address world problems? I

DOI: 10.4324/9781003212881-8

am not suggesting some Pollyannaish notion that we would all be sitting around singing Kumbaya or that we would become superheroes, but that showing up with the C² Factor in our back pocket positions us to be much more effective.

When we listen to the news about the Middle East, about vaccination hesitation or inadequate distribution, or fires in California and Greece, or trafficking of young girls, what mindset do we bring? If we show up to every minute of our lives with the mindset of C², the world becomes a place with imminently more potential for change.

We also must show up with courage as well as curiosity. Courage means taking action. We've talked about how we can take action to improve conditions as individuals, as team members and leaders, as heads of organizations responsible for their culture. So, what if we want to take action expressly to make the world a better place? How can we do that? We need to channel the energy that curiosity inspires.

HEROES WITH SUPER C² FACTOR

I interviewed over 60 leaders, all champions with powerful stories of applying curiosity and courage in their personal and professional lives. I listened to many compelling stories of individuals who seemed to have embraced the imperative of the C² Factor from early in life to overcome obstacles that would have defeated others. Occasionally, I heard a story of personal and professional curiosity and courage that was staggering in its breadth and depth. Imrana Jalai is one of those heroines I was honored to interview who has made it her mission to apply her C² Factor to improving the world.

Long before Imrana joined the World Bank as Chair of the Inspection Panel investigating complaints about adverse impacts of the Bank's projects and investments in the far corners of the developing world, she wielded both her curiosity and courage with a tenacity and fortitude seen only in those rare, special individuals who can claim the C² Factor as their own superpower. As a prelude to her many accomplishments, Imrana, as a 5-year-old little girl, relentlessly asked her strict, Muslim father "why," challenging his responses and seeking more freedoms. Thus began the pattern of her life using her endless curiosity and unwavering courage to seek out injustices and find ways to right the wrongs.

Becoming a lawyer and a renowned human rights lawyer, Imrana has spent decades understanding the intricacies of the many ways women are disadvantaged and discriminated against in her native Fiji and throughout the Pacific Islands. And she has taken courageous action to mitigate those inequities and fight for justice. She has been arrested, prosecuted, harassed, and even threatened with physical violence as she fought corruption and spoke up against military coups in support of democracy and the law of the land.

Imrana founded the Fijian Women's Right Movement and the UNICEF award-winning organization, The Pacific Regional Rights Resource Team, authored *Law for Pacific Women: A Legal Rights Handbook*, and is the architect of the Fiji Family Law Act providing Fijian women unprecedented rights in the country.

Her's is a lifetime of obvious achievement, but perhaps not as obvious is its underpinning of ceaseless curiosity tightly interwoven with what, at times, is staggering courage. The C^2 Factor is not simply a tool Imrana accesses in specific situations. It is embedded in her approach to every facet of her life providing greater satisfaction, effectiveness, and meaning.

In a different but related sphere is the heroism of Yael Eisenstat. Yael has worked around the globe as a CIA officer, a White House advisor, a diplomat, the head of a global risk firm, and was the Global Head of Elections Integrity Operations for political advertising at Facebook. That is, until she was fired.

She was hired in 2018 as Facebook attempted to dig out from the public relations crisis around Cambridge Analytica's improper use of the site's data and Russia's use of the platform to interfere in the 2016 presidential election. After only two days on the job, her title and job description changed, and she was sidelined for questioning why Facebook was not fact checking political ads and for trying to help ensure that attempts at voter suppression wasn't occurring through those ads. When she asked to be moved to where she could do her job, she was fired.

When I asked her about the experience, she told me, "It's so weird because this is a company that really loves to promote itself all about free expression and connecting people and my boss literally told me that they didn't want me asking questions."

What makes her more of a heroine however was her decline of a severance package. Taking the money would have required her to sign a nondisclosure agreement that included a non-disparagement clause written so broadly that she would have been barred, forever, from saying anything negative about the company, its products, any individuals who work there, and even the terms of her employment. Instead, she continues to work and be a public advocate for transparency and accountability in technology, particularly where real-world consequences affect democracy and societies around the world.

BUT FOR US MORTALS …

I am humbled when I hear stories like Imrana's and Yael's. I am inspired, but I know that my life is not on those trajectories. So, what can those of us who have the C² Factor but are mere mortals do to manifest our courage as well as our curiosity? We could demonstrate, march on Washington, write petitions and letters to the editor, etc. While those actions may be somewhat meritorious, by a single individual they are likely to have limited impact.

1. Prosocial Organizations

There is, of course, no need to be a lone wolf. There are a number of different types of organizational structures that enable participation in prosocial activities. The form of these structures dictates the types of undertakings they conduct, and the challenges vary, but all must engage curiosity and courage to be effective.

Perhaps the most common model of prosocial endeavors by corporations is the Corporate Social Responsibility, CSR model. In addition to corporate philanthropy, in this model, businesses pledge to operate in a way that promotes community welfare and the environment as well as directing a portion of their profits toward charitable work. The charitable work is an add-on to the core business and works in part to enhance the corporate brand. Toms, Warby Parker, and Newman's Own are examples of this model.

The challenge for the champion leader in this situation is to use the C² Factor to examine closely how projects are selected, what the underlying assumptions are about their purpose, and what unintended consequences might there be to any undertaking. This may involve killing someone's sacred cow charity.

Next on the continuum of corporate prosocial models is the Benefit Corporations and the certified B-Corps that make social responsibility part of their core mission. These organizations commit to transparency and accountability as they align business decisions with their impact on shareholders, employees, customers, the community, and the local and global environments.

While Starbuck's is not officially in this group, its practices conform to their values. In 2018, the leadership of Starbucks demonstrated the C² Factor in the way they handled the racial incident that occurred at one of their stores. Two black men were handcuffed and arrested by Philadelphia police after they asked to use the bathroom without having made a purchase. Senior leaders met with community leaders and Starbucks partners to understand what had happened. Six weeks after the incident, they closed 8,000 stores to provide its 175,000 employees with training geared to preventing discrimination. They not only had the curiosity to learn from the people involved as well as from experts on racial bias, but they also had the courage to confront it head-on.

Twelve years ago, when I was looking for a way to give back, I had trouble choosing a cause. I cared about a lot of different issues – health, environment, social welfare – all spoke to me, none singularly. There are over 1.6 million charities in the United States and over 675 in the Washington, DC, area alone. I couldn't choose. Around the same time, a friend of mine invited me to come to a Rotary meeting. I have to admit, I went reluctantly. Why would I bother with a group of old White men sitting around drinking coffee? But I liked the idea that they supported a variety of different charities, so I agreed to attend.

2. Not Your Father's Rotary

I couldn't have been more wrong about Rotary. The club I joined 12 years ago is 60% women, 37% people of color, and 70% under age 64. Every meeting I attend I learn something which fuels my curiosity, and I am inspired by the courage of others.

Moreover, Rotary is an international organization with 35,000 clubs in more than 220 geographic regions and 340,000 members in the United States alone. The organization has a seat in the General Assembly of the United Nations in recognition of the efforts of its membership to foster goodwill and peace across national boundaries. In addition, it holds the highest consultative status offered to a nongovernmental organization by the UN's Economic and Social Council, which oversees many specialized UN agencies.

Rotary projects range in size from $150 million to eradicate polio worldwide to local community projects of a couple of thousand dollars. With a mission including six humanitarian mandates: promote peace, fight disease, provide clean water, save mothers and children, support education, and grow local economies, their projects range in scope from the global to the local community.

Among its largest projects, Rotary International was a founding partner of the Global Polio Eradication Initiative that reduced polio cases by 99.9%. At the other end of the spectrum – local and smaller, but still powerful – is Kids In Need Distributors (KIND) founded by Jeremy Lichtenstein, a real estate agent and Rotary member.

Jeremy discovered that despite living in one of the richest counties in the United States, over 34% of the public school students were on the Federal Free and Reduced Meal Plan. Over 50,00 children live in families who do not have enough money to feed everyone. The FARM plan provided these children with free or reduced cost breakfast and lunch every school day, but there is no FARM plan to feed these kids on the weekends or the summer.

So, Jeremy started KIND. In the beginning, he was the entire workforce. Working with just one elementary school, he began making trips to the grocery store and dropping off weekend food supplies for students. A warmhearted guy, Jeremy's curiosity about those children inspired him to understand their circumstances and he needed courage to stand up to bureaucracies and attitudes that initially stood in his way:

> I would go to the schools and tell them that I had $15,000 worth of food and they told me they didn't have space for us to pack the bags! It was a challenge. I had to stand up to corporate sponsors who wanted to participate but wanted "credit" for it – pictures with the kids or logos on the backpacks for example. I insisted that the recipients have their privacy and dignity and turned down those sponsors.

Today KIND has 170 volunteers who every six weeks make trips to a local store, where they purchase, and then transport carloads full of nonperishable food to schools. There, school personnel, volunteers, and students work together to discreetly drop bags of food into kids' backpacks.

Having discussed various nonprofit structures in which we can engage our C² Factor for doing good in the world, I want to circle back to business and how one can have a prosocial mission and still make a profit.

APPLYING THE C² FACTOR IN A HUMANITARIAN START-UP

1. The Poop Story

Picture a long line of tanker trucks winding along highways bringing human sewage to treatment facilities. Think of the amount of fuel it takes, the amount of pollution it creates, and the congestion on the roadways. Imagine seeing raw sewage being pumped into rivers while only feet away children swim and people wash. Picture teenage girls having to wait until nighttime to have enough privacy to use public latrines but then being in danger of sexual assault. Picture having to defecate in the street because there is no other option. Imagine that you have dysentery from polluted water and no place to relieve yourself. Those were the pictures in Diana Yousef's mind when she started her business.

Diana told me that she is "wired like a scientist" who wanted "to solve problems that really matter to people." Her parents come from Egypt, a still-developing country, so she was curious about how she could help people find solutions for challenges that in the United States we take for granted. After earning a PhD in biochemistry and structural biology and spending some time in academia, she went to Columbia Business School so that she could learn to apply "the tools of science and the power of nature to solve problems for people in the developing world."

When I interviewed her about starting her business, change:WATER Labs, she told me, "At the time I didn't feel courageous. I was actually quite scared and desperate, but curiosity drove me. I was never good at doing something that was already figured out. I needed to be trying something new."

Diana's company has developed two patent-pending technologies to get rid of waste onsite: (a) an evaporative material that quickly shrinks human waste by converting ~90–95% of it into pure water vapor; (b) a pee-powered bio-battery that turns urine into electricity. Her inventions dramatically alter those images of caravans of waste trucks and unsafe public latrines in developing economies.

Diana says that investors often ask her what it is her company is doing differently than another well-known foundation in this space. Her answer is, "I think we approached it from a more humble standpoint. We asked questions of the people who needed this solution upfront as opposed to assuming that we knew. We were curious and eager to learn."

Along the way, Diana faced a number of obstacles requiring her to call upon her C² Factor. Early on she discovered that her two partners had lost faith in her idea and left to pursue another business without her. *"I had to ask myself what I was going to do - accept that I was going to fail or double down and see if I could make it happen."* She called on her courage and moved on.

Then again in 2018, while traveling the world seeking investment, the company had a technological setback.

> We were running out of money. We were having technology challenges. I was dealing with a couple of really difficult investor negotiations. I had been very transparent with these investors and told them I wouldn't sign anything or take their money until I figured out whether I could solve the problem. We did get over it, get beyond it in a better way, but by that point, I think they were spooked.

Instead of telling her directly, however, the potential investors dragged her through a long process, asking for draconian terms and in the end, at the last moment backed out of the deal:

> I literally had a hundred dollars left in my bank account. I felt on one hand that it probably was a good thing because they're not good faith actors but on the other hand, I had people on the payroll depending on me.

Diana lent her personal money to the company and began negotiations for a large, prestigious grant with no idea of her chances of receiving it. She endured three tortuous months, went through a difficult delivery of her third child, and decided that she needed to set a limit:

> I told myself, if that money doesn't come in, I'm closing down. I'll have to write off all that money that I lent to the company. I just can't do this anymore. The money landed the day before my drop-dead date.

Today's change:WATER Labs has installed the first set of toilets in Uganda next to the neonatal unit of a hospital and a girls' school. The "no odor success" confirmed its applicability for high-density, crowded communities. A new prototype is being deployed in Panama which if goes as planned, will bring sanitation to tens of thousands who currently have no hope of such facilities. CWL[1] is in talks with six additional countries in Latin America and Asia as it prepares for the commercial launch.

Diana says:

> I remind myself that you can't predict the future. You don't know; you just have to be okay with whatever comes and do what you can today and be okay with whatever outcome tomorrow. Maybe that's how curiosity and courage interplays. Curiosity is just keeping an open mind to what is going to happen and the courage to say, "it'll be fine."

2. Social Entrepreneurs Need the C² Factor

Diana is a special breed of entrepreneurs who wants to make profits while doing good in the world. Called "social entrepreneurs," David Bornstein[2] says of them, "What business entrepreneurs are to the economy, social entrepreneurs are to social change." Often through technology advances, social entrepreneurs bring innovative solutions to concerns in the areas of the environmental, health, education, housing, and other social welfare challenges. Renewable energy solutions, microfinance firms, and clean water efforts are examples of social entrepreneurs' enterprises.

Muhammad Yunus[3] founded Grameen Bank based on the techniques of microfinancing. This organization is designed to empower villagers with the funds they need to develop financial self-sufficiency. It has a loan payback rate of 98%, which is higher than any traditional bank. For this pioneering work, Yunus was awarded the Nobel Prize in 2006, U.S. Presidential Medal of Freedom in 2009, and the Congressional Gold Medal in 2010.

SafePoint Trust introduced a nonreusable, inexpensive syringe in 2006 to be used in underfunded clinics. This innovation safeguards against the transmission of blood-borne diseases. The company, founded by Mark Koska,[4] has delivered over 4 billion safe injections in 40 countries by Auto-Disable (AD) syringes. In 2015, The Schwab Foundation Social

Entrepreneurs of the Year listed Koska for his pioneering solution to world health issues.

In 2013, Kate Jakubas[5] founded Meliora Cleaning Products, a sustainable company which produces laundry soap and other household cleaning products without chemical toxins, eliminating the negative impact that these products have on personal health and the environment.

This website lists 50 social entrepreneurs: https://growensemble.com /social-entrepreneurs/ and the following website lists numerous social entrepreneur enterprises devoted to renewable energy: https://greenfuture .io/solar/social-entrepreneurship-renewable-energy.

Poverty, the environment, health and wellness, equity, and community stability are a few of the problems that social entrepreneurs might address, but trying to create sustainable solutions seems like trying to bail out the ocean with a teaspoon. They are multifaceted, complex problems involving millions of people, contradictory opinions, and requiring burdensome resources – economic and otherwise. That is why in the 1960s, Horst Rittel,[6] a design theorist, described them as "wicked problems." Yet these are the very problems that prosocial organizations and social entrepreneurs attempt to address and why the C² Factor is essential to these endeavors.

So, what methodology might we use if we want to ensure that the C² Factor is being incorporated into social entrepreneurship or for that matter any of the spheres we have discussed? Design thinking is an excellent choice. Conceived by Stanford University's d-school, design thinking is probably best known for its commercial use, brought to the market by the design company, IDEO.

DESIGN THINKING AND THE C² FACTOR: ONE MARRIAGE MADE IN HEAVEN

The term "design thinking" was first coined by David Kelly, the founder of Stanford University's d-school. In 1991 he, along with Tim Brown,[7] co-founded IDEO, a design firm that initially focused on products for business and brought the concept of design thinking to the mainstream. The approach was further popularized by Time Brown's 2009 book, *Change by Design: How Design Thinking Transforms Organizations and Inspires Innovation.*

While there have been many iterations, elaborations, and modifications of the design thinking process over the years, they share common factors all of which are at their essence curiosity and courage based.

Design thinking is a way of approaching problems that is based in a deep understanding of the people for whom the products or services are designed and the problems they face. Coming from a place of profound curiosity, design thinkers don't simply ask people what they want, they observe people in their daily lives and along with cultural interpreters and guides, imagine how they could provide improvements. An example of this in the business world is the idea of mobile phones which before we had them, we didn't know we needed them.

A central premise in design thinking is asking questions and challenging assumptions, a manifestation of curiosity and courage that we have discussed before. And as discussed in Chapter 5, design thinkers go beyond the presenting problem and look for root causes.

The third step in design thinking is to "ideate," that is, to brainstorm as many solutions as possible without prejudging them. Once generated, team members are encouraged to challenge them and try to find the obstacles that might prevent them from being successfully implemented. Finally, prototypes are created that are tested and modified as the results indicate are necessary. Design thinkers have the courage to execute their ideas without the need to defend them but rather to welcome criticism intended to improve the outcomes and pivot their approach when necessary.

The ideal member of a design thinking team has been described as action-oriented and "T-shaped," meaning they have expert knowledge of a particular subject but are also curious, open, and empathetic about other's perspectives. That is, they have a high C^2 Factor. Interestingly, Tim Brown and Jocelyn Wyatt[8] in their paper on design thinking and social innovation assert that the biggest impediment to adopting design thinking is the fear of failure, demonstrating why both elements of the C^2 Factor are crucial.[9]

Whatever methodology you use for encouraging, building, and embedding innovation in your organization – whether you're implementing Skunk Works giving a high degree of autonomy and reducing the bureaucracy for your engineering teams (https://lockheedmartin.com/en-us/whow-we-are/business-areas/aeronautics/skunkworks.html), rapid prototyping to iterate and get critical feedback, agile methodologies to scale, lean start-up to experiment, The Disney Way or the De Bono Way – it's clear the C^2 Factor will be the key to success. Curiosity to think outside the boxes and really listen. Courage to try something new and accept the critique. The champion leadership skill to do it again!

CONCLUSION

We are all born with curiosity and the capacity for courage. Whether those traits grow and develop or become inhibited has a lot to do with our experiences. Early in our lives, our parents, teachers, friends, coaches, and others can encourage us to be open and eager to learn about everything around us or discourage us by insisting that we simply accept what is immediately in front of us. We can see the influential people around us model courage and urge us to take judicious risks or we can hear admonishments to put safety above all else. So too the organizations we are members of as adults – religious, community, professional – can either constrain or foster these qualities. Nonetheless, we all have the ability to strengthen these traits and activate them to improve our lives and the lives of those around us.

When both curiosity and courage are highly developed, they have a special alchemy, they intensify each other and become what I have called the C² Factor. Champion leaders, those most able to develop and sustain robust organizations even in these turbulent times, know how to engage their C² Factor. Sometimes relying more on their curiosity, to keep them in touch with the world beyond their immediate environment, for example, and sometimes on their courage as they make decisions and take actions to guide the ship through a sea of uncertainty such as we face today. Sometimes the action of the C² Factor is more obvious than others, for example, when leaders ask for and listen to honest critiques of their ideas.

You are likely already a champion leader or headed that way. You have been curious and courageous in your life, but you may not have named them as such. You may not have recognized them as the signature traits that differentiate champion leaders from the merely adequate. And, most likely, you have never taken steps to strengthen those muscles and use them in a deliberate way in every facet of your life. With the pressures of daily life, it is easy to be consumed with those things that seemingly must be done now and thus we fail to lift our heads up and anticipate the future or to be curious about our situation, the environment, and the world around us. How many assumptions are we making about ourselves, our partners, and the problems we face that need reexamining? What knowledge do we think we have that we can deepen or reconsider? What action do we need to take that we've been delaying? What conversation have we been avoiding? We need the C^2 Factor to answer these.

When we become conscious of the C^2 Factor, we access it more easily and apply it as the situation calls for. And each time we engage the C^2 Factor, we strengthen it. If we pay attention to the opportunities around us to show up this way, we see that they are plentiful. Recognizing others who have accomplished so much by engaging these traits, we can intentionally emulate them.

You needn't be slaying dragons in the world or engaging the C^2 Factor 24/7 to be a champion leader. Whether it's simply gaining the ability to diffuse group tensions with curiosity, build consensus among teams, speaking up for issues or individuals, advocating for innovation in your organizations, or volunteering some of your time, your effectiveness and fulfillment will be enhanced by your curiosity and courage.

In addition, curiosity and courage help us live more satisfying and fulfilling lives. Experiencing the world with curiosity allows us to never be bored. When we look around us at the world and our place in it with curiosity, there is so much to know and if we have courage, there is so much to do. By identifying the C^2 Factor and how it is essential to thriving in all the arenas of our lives – personal, one-to-one relationships, team membership, leadership at all levels of our organizations, and the broader world, we can more purposefully embrace it, nurture it, and exercise it. I hope this book has been an inspiration for you to claim your strengths and put them to use for all of us.

NOTES

1. CWL's evaporative approach to "flushing" mimics how plants use evapotranspiration to pull moisture from soil, releasing it as pure molecular water through stomata on their leaves. Inspired by nature's recycling of waste into energy, CWL's bio-battery uses symbiotic microbes to collaboratively consume and convert urine into electricity. www.change-water.com

2. Bornstein, David. *How to Change the World: Social Entrepreneurs and the Power of New Ideas.* Oxford, England: Oxford University Press; 2nd edition (September 17, 2007).

3. https://www.nobelprize.org/prizes/peace/2006/grameen/facts/.

4. https://charitydigital.org.uk/topics/topics/bitesized-insight-marc-koska-safepoint-trust-2928.

5. https://growensemble.com/meliora-kate-jakubas/.

6. https://www.interaction-design.org/literature/article/design-thinking-get-a-quick-overview-of-the-history.

7. Brown, Tim. *Change by Design: How Design Thinking Transforms Organizations and Inspires Innovation.* Revised, Updated edition. New York: Harper Business, 2009.

8. Brown, Tim, and Wyatt, Jocelyn. "Design Thinking for Social Innovation." *Stanford Innovation Review* (Winter 2010). https://ssir.org/articles/entry/design_thinking_for_social_innovation#

9. As commissioned by the Bill and Melinda Gates Foundation in 2008 and maintained by IDEO, a roadmap for applying designer thinking to a project can be found free of charge at: https://www.designkit.org/resources.

Index

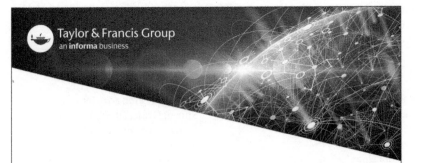